# USE CASE LEVELS OF TEST

*INNOVATE & WORK SMART IN SOFTWARE TEST DESIGN*

# CONTENTS

# INNOVATION & WORKING SMARTER IN TEST DESIGN

In my book – Succeeding with Use Cases: Working Smart to Deliver Quality – I noted that *innovation* and *ways of working smarter* often arise when ideas from multiple areas are combined, suggesting future improvements in use case-driven development might likely come from the cross-pollination of use cases with other disciplines of software engineering. Whereas that book took a broad but shallow approach – the synergy from uses cases coupled with a smorgasbord of software disciplines – this book takes a deep dive into one area where cross-pollination has already taken place: software testing.

This book presents a strategy for software test design based on the idea of use case levels of test combined with high bang for the buck ideas from software testing, quality function deployment (QFD), software reliability's operational profiles, structured analysis and design's C.R.U.D. matrix, and formal methods like model-based specification and discrete math for testers. The goal of this "cross-pollination" is to provide you the tester with a test design strategy to

- Evaluate a set of use cases for test adequacy, determining if you are missing any essential for testing
- Budget test design time to maximize reliability and minimize testing cost
- Strike a balance between breadth of coverage of all use cases and depth of coverage for the most frequently used, critical use cases.
- Provide a step by step process for when to use the plethora of test techniques covered in so many testing books helping address the plea "Just tell me where to start!"
- Decompose the big problem of test design for a whole system or application into manageable chunks by using levels of test – not of units, modules or subsystems – but paths through the system
- Introduce innovative test design techniques not covered in other testing books; elaborate on key techniques covered only briefly in other books

Let me review here the disciplines that I see as having "cross-pollinated" to make this book, and in general touch on what I see as this book's value added to the set of books we already have on testing.

## OPERATIONAL PROFILES

In John Musa's Amazon review of my first book he commented: *"I have always felt that there were many fruitful relationships between use cases and software reliability engineering".* To me, operational profiles and use cases seem such a natural fit.

Operational Profiles (from software reliability engineering; used here to help budget time in test design) have been discussed in a few other testing books but none that I'm aware discussing their integration with use case based testing as presented here, or to the depth discussed here. See for example QFD next.

## QFD

Quality function deployment or QFD (from requirements engineering; used here for test prioritization) appeared in my first book and spurred a lot of interest. This book's presentation of generating an operational profile from a use case diagram via a QFD matrix is, as far as I'm aware, unique.

## C.R.U.D.

The C.R.U.D. matrix (from structured analysis and design; used here to help with determining test adequacy of a set of use cases) has been covered in a few testing books and use case books. In this book I've tried to expand upon their use as described in these other books, as well as showing how to leverage an operational profile and C.R.U.D. matrix to help spot high risk data entities in the system or application.

## FORMAL METHODS, DISCRETE MATH FOR TESTERS

Al Davis' software development principle #28: *"Know Formal Methods .. their use (even on the back of an envelope) can aid significantly in uncovering problems .. At least one person on every project should be comfortable with formal methods to ensure that opportunities for building quality into the product are not lost".*[1]

---

[1] *201 Principles of Software Development* by Alan Davis, McGraw-Hill, 1995

And why shouldn't that "at least one person" be a *tester*?![2] The formal methods community has long been concerned with test design, as indicated for example by panels such as the one I was on in 1996 asking the question "Formal methods and testing: why the state-of-the art is not the state-of-the practice"[3]

The approach discussed in this book of pairing light-weight, "back of an envelope" style, model-based specification and discrete math with use case scenario operations feels like a natural fit to me, and jives with Al Davis' principle #28.

This topic was covered in the last book, prompted some questions on how to expand the techniques while keeping it practical, so I've borrowed on and expanded on it in this book. I see the approach advocated in this book – selective use of these techniques on high risk operations of high risk use cases to *augment* use cases (but not replace! Al Davis' principle #54[4]) - as a practical approach to helping close the gap between state-of-the art and practice in testing.

Discrete math for testers (sets, relations, Venn diagrams) has been covered by a number of testing books. They are powerful tools for testers, but getting across their *practical application* is in my opinion a shortcoming in many testing books. In this book I've tried to give them a very *"Here's how to use them"* approach via lots of examples.

Prolog (Programming in Logic) came on the scene in the early 70s as a programming language popular for tackling problems in artificial intelligence like problem solving, natural language understanding (think *syntax* as in syntax testing), and rule-based expert systems. And the formal methods testing community recognized its potential as a tool to aid in test design. I've included one such example in this book, illustrating its use to sanity check that a syntax definition of an input to

---

[2] Jorgensen, in *Software Testing: A Craftsman's Approach*, argues "More than any other life cycle activity, testing lends itself to mathematical descriptions and analysis".
[3] Formal Methods and Testing: Why the State-of-the Art is Not the State-of-the Practice, ACM SIGSOFT, Software Engineering Notes vol. 21 no 4, July 1996, p64.
[4] Principle #54: "Augment, never replace, natural language ... In fact, one good idea is to keep the natural language and more formal specification side-by-side ... do a manual check between the two to verify conformity.." *201 Principles of Software Development*, Alan Davis.

be used for testing actually says what we *think* it says, then to help write tests by acting like a "code coverage" tool, but for syntax rules.

## A DEEPER DIVE ON SOME COMMONLY DISCUSSED TESTING TECHNIQUES

There are some topics covered here that have been covered in nearly every testing book written. For such areas I try to provide the 20/80 you need to know (so the book is fairly stand-alone) with pointers to other existing sources if you want to do further reading. But *additionally*, I try to provide some different angles on these topics.

For example, it's probably the case that no other topic in testing has been written about as much as equivalence partitioning and boundary value analysis. But it's also the case that most books use a simple numeric input to explain equivalence partitioning and boundary value analysis. So I've tried to add value on these well-discussed topics by taking on more complicated problems.

One example, syntax testing is a common problem in input testing, and recursive rule definitions a common way to describe many inputs. Yet few books tackle the problem of black-box test design from such recursive definitions of syntax. In this book we'll take on syntax testing of such inputs using the example of internet keyword search queries.

## USE CASE LEVELS OF TEST

Last but certainly not least is the idea of use case levels of test. Use cases as a basis for test design have been discussed by a number of books,  but at this writing the strategy presented here based on four levels of use case test is, as far as I'm aware, unique (for example generating an operational profile from a use case diagram; working with preconditions, postconditions and invariants at the operation level).

Use case levels of test provide the framework that hopefully helps address that plea so often uttered by testers and organizations starting to climb the testing learning curve: "Just tell me where to start!". And augmented with operational profiles use case levels of test are key to budgeting time wisely in test design.

So, this book is the accumulation of thoughts, conference papers, white-papers, training classes and slide presentations I've done over the years explaining to others

– as well as helping myself come to grips with – a *framework* built around use cases for leveraging a wealth of testing techniques, as well as techniques from other software disciplines, for innovation and a way of working smarter in software test design.

## WORKING SMARTER: A STRATEGY TO BETTER BUDGET TEST DESIGN TIME

Every student in school – from elementary to graduate – is familiar with the angst of taking tests, hearing the dreaded line "Times up, put your pencils down!", followed by the that feeling of regret as you think "If only I hadn't spent so much time on that one question!"

I'd like you to consider that writing tests for software is a bit like taking tests in school. Both are tasks typically done in a finite, allotted amount of time, so it's best to have a strategy for using your time wisely, and knowing what techniques work well (or don't!) on various problem types.

One of the key goals of this book is to provide you – the tester tasked with designing tests for a system or application – a strategy for approaching test design so that when you hear **"Times up, put your pencils down!"**, you can relax knowing you budgeted your time wisely.

My assumption is that you are a tester or test manager working in a software development shop where use cases have been used in-whole or in-part to specify the system or application for which you've been tasked to write tests, or alternatively you are familiar enough with use cases to write them as proxy tests before starting real test design (I'll explain the importance of the role of use cases in this strategy shortly).

And I assume you have a fixed amount of time in which to get tests written, hence prioritizing and budgeting test design time is important.

The question then is: *Where do you start?!*

One approach would be bottom-up[5]: jump in feet first with some use case and start writing test cases using every conceivable test design technique you are familiar with.

13

The problem with this approach? When the clock runs out on test design, there's a very good chance you've written too many tests, or the wrong granularity of tests, for some use cases and not enough – maybe none? – for many others (say the ones used most frequently). Also, the bottom-up approach, focusing solely on individual use cases, may lead you to neglect the testing of use cases that should be tested in concert, i.e. integration tested. And finally, what's to say the use cases you started with were an adequate base from which to design tests in the first place, e.g. is there some part of the system that won't get tested because a use case was not provided?

An alternate approach is to

- First evaluate the use cases as a whole for *test adequacy*; determine if you are missing any use cases essential for adequate testing.
- Next budget test design time for each use case, a technique often referred to in planning as timeboxing. But rather than an arbitrary allocation of time (say equal time for all), budget time based on an operational profile: an analysis of the high traffic paths through your system. This allows you, the test designer, to concentrate on the most frequently used use cases; those having a greater chance of failure in the hands of the user.
- Then for each use case, design tests top-down, level by level (I'll explain this shortly) applying the test design techniques that work well at each level (covered in this book), adjusting the rigor of test design (again, covered in this book) to match the time budgeted each use case. This top-down, level by level approach means you will produce coarser grain tests first, finer grain tests later as time permits. This, coupled with time budgets per use case based on an operational profile, will help strike the balance between breadth of coverage of all use cases and depth of coverage for the use cases most frequently used.

---

[5] I'll be using the terms "bottom-up" and "top-down", but do *not* mean this as used to describe strategies for integration testing. It is used here solely in terms of use case levels of test being described, and how to come at the problem of test design.

So this book is organized around just such a strategy so that when the clock runs out – **"Time's up! Put your pencils down!"** – you can relax knowing you have spent test design time wisely.

Use cases play a key role in the "working smart" strategy presented in this book; let's see why.

## USE CASES: COMPROMISE BETWEEN AD HOC AND "REAL TESTS"

Part of the reason use cases have gained the attention they have in testing is that they are already pretty close to what testers often write for test cases.

One of the leaders in the testing tool arena is HP's Quality Center (formerly Mercury Test Director). The example test shown in Figure 0-1 is part of a Quality Center tutorial in which the tester is instructed that *"After you add a test ... you define test steps -- detailed, step-by-step instructions ... A step includes the actions to be performed on your application and the expected results"*. As the example illustrates, anyone comfortable with writing use cases would be comfortable writing tests in Quality Center, and vice versa.

| Details | Design Steps | Test Script | Attachments | Req Coverage | Linked Defects |
|---------|--------------|-------------|-------------|--------------|----------------|

| Step Name | Description | Expected Result |
|-----------|-------------|-----------------|
| 1.Display the cruise special page | click the cruises button | the cruise special page opens |
| 2.display the cruise reservation page | click the now accepting reservations button | the cruise reservation page opens |
| 3.book the cruise | enter passenger name, credit card information, and address. click ok. | the cruise confirmation page opens. |
| 4.print cruise confirmation | click the print button | a confirmation page is printed. |
| 5.log off. | click the sign-off button | returns to the sign-on page |

Figure 0-1 Test design in HP's Quality Center is very use case scenario like.

As has been pointed out by others, the early availability of use cases written by a development team gives testers a good head start on test design. What this means

15

for our strategy is that, in a pinch (you've run out of time for test design) use cases provide a good compromise between ad hoc testing and full blown test cases.

On the one hand, ad hoc testing carries the risks of unplanned, undocumented (can't peer review; not repeatable) testing that depends solely on the improvisation of the tester to find bugs. On the other hand we have full-fledged test cases for which even Beizer, a proponent of "real testing" vs. "kiddie testing", has said *"If every test designer had to analyze and predict the expected behavior for every test case for every component, then test design would be very expensive"*.

So use cases provide a good balance between the informal and formal. By starting test design from a set of use cases a test team can design full-fledged test cases as time permits from the most important use cases, and for the rest allow testers to "pound away" on and off the happy path; a sort of controlled ad hoc testing where use cases provide some order to the otherwise unplanned and undocumented testing.

## *USE CASE LEVELS OF TEST*

Another facet of use cases key to the strategy presented in this book is a way to decompose a big problem (say, write tests for a system) into smaller problems (e.g. test the preconditions on a critical operation) by using use case levels of test.

So what do I mean by use case levels of test? Most testers are familiar with the concept of levels of test such as systems test (the testing of a whole system, i.e. all assembled units), integration test (testing two or more units together), or unit test (testing a unit standalone). Uses cases provide a way to decompose test design into levels of test as well, not based on units, *but rather on increasingly finer granularity paths through the system.*

The parts of this book are organized around four levels of use case test design, and I'll be using the analogy of the "View from 30,000 feet" to illustrate the role of use case levels to zoom from the big-picture (the major interstate highways through your application) down to discrete operations that form the steps of a use case scenario. This is illustrated in Figure 0-2.

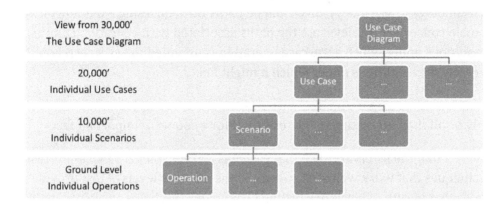

Figure 0-2 Use cases levels of test: zooming from the big picture to the detailed

Let's start with the view of the system from 30,000 feet: the use case diagram. At this level the system is a set of actors, interacting with a system, described as a set of use cases. This is the coarsest level of paths through your system; the collection of major interstate highways of your system.

Dropping down to the 20,000-foot view we have the individual use case itself, typically viewed as a particular "happy path"[6] through the system, with associated branches, some being not so happy paths. In other words, a use case is a collection of related paths – each called a scenario -- through the system.

From there we drop to the 10,000-foot view which zooms in on a particular scenario of a use case, i.e. one path through a use case. While a scenario represents a single path through the system from a black-box perspective, different inputs to the same scenario very likely cause the underlying code to execute differently; there are multiple paths through the single scenario at the code level.

And finally, at ground level we reach discrete operations; the finest granularity action / re-action of the dance between actor and system. These are what make up the steps of a scenario. At this level paths are through the code implementing an operation. If dealing with an application or system implemented using object-

---

[6] If you are unfamiliar with this term, the "happy path" of a use case is the default scenario, or path, through the use case, generally free of exceptions or errors.

oriented technology (quite likely), this could be paths through a single method on an object. A main concern at this level are the paths associated with operation failures; testing conditions under which a use case operation is intended to work correctly, and conversely the conditions under which it might fail.

The fact that use cases provide an alternate way to view levels of test wouldn't necessarily be all that interesting to the tester but for a couple of important facts.

First is the fact that the levels are such that each has certain standard black-box test design techniques that work well at that level. So the use case levels of test provide a way to index that wealth of black-box testing techniques; this helps answer that plea of "Just tell me where to start!".

Second, for each use case level of test, the "path through a system" metaphor affords a way to prioritize where you do test design at that level, e.g. spending more time on the paths most frequently traveled by the user or that touch critical data.

## How to use the Parts of This Book

There are four parts to this book, organized around the four levels of use case test illustrated in Figure 0-2. These use case levels of test provide a sort of road map on how to approach test design for a system, working top-down from the 30,000-foot view to ground level. The bit of pseudo code below in Figure 0-3 illustrates a strategy for using the parts of the book.

---

Apply **Part I** to the Use Case Diagram. This produces a test adequate set of prioritized use cases with budgeted test design time for each, as well as integration tests for the set

For each use case U from the previous step, *until budgeted time for U expires* do:

- Apply **Part II** to use case U to produce a set of tests to cover it's scenarios
- For each test T from the previous step, *in priority order* of the scenario T covers do:
    - Apply **Part III** to test T creating additional tests based on inputs and combinations of inputs
    - Apply **Part IV** to any critical operations in test T producing additional tests based on preconditions, postconditions and invariants

---

Figure 0-3 Pseudo code for use of parts of the book

Because parts II-IV are timeboxed according to the operational profile (notice the phrase "until budgeted time expires") this strategy will produce more tests for use cases frequently used. This is the key contribution from the field of software reliability engineering to maximize quality while minimizing testing costs.

This strategy is graphically depicted in Figure 0-4. Numbers refer to the parts – 1 through 4 -- of this book.

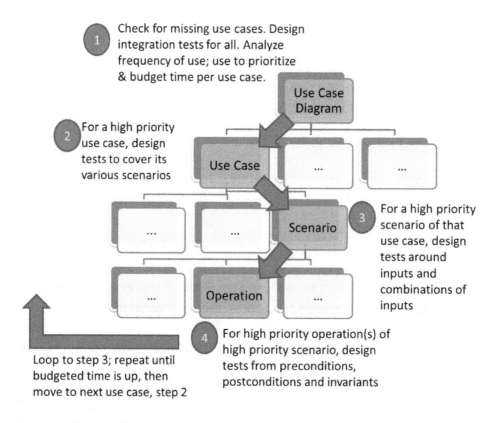

Figure 0-4 Strategy for working through the use case levels of test

Let's walk through each part of the book and see what will be covered.

## PART I USE CASE DIAGRAM

Part I of the book starts with the view of the system from 30,000 feet: the use case diagram. At this level the system is a set of actors, interacting with a system, described as set of use cases. Paths through the system are in terms of traffic trod across a whole set of use cases, those belonging to the use case diagram

As tests at lower levels will be based on these use cases, it makes sense to begin by asking: Is the use case diagram missing any use cases essential for adequate testing? This is addressed in Chapter 1 where we look at the use of a C.R.U.D. matrix, a tool allowing you to judge test adequacy by how well the use cases of the use case diagram cover the data life-cycle of entities in your system. Not only does the

C.R.U.D. matrix test the adequacy of the use case diagram, it is essentially a high level test case for the entire system, providing expected inputs (read), and outputs (create, update, delete) for the entire system in a compact succinct form.

Still working at the use case diagram level, in Chapter 2 we look at another tool – the operational profile – as a way to help you, the tester, concentrate on the most frequently used use cases, and hence those having a greater chance of failure in the hands of the user. The chapter describes how to construct an operational profile from the use case diagram, and the use of an operational profile as a way to prioritize use cases; budget test design time per use case; spot "high risk" data; and design load and stress tests.

Chapter 3 wraps up our look at testing at the use case diagram level by introducing techniques for *testing the use cases in concert*, i.e. integration testing of the use cases.

## PART II THE USE CASE

Part II drops us down to the 20,000-foot view where we have the individual use case itself. At this level of test paths through the system are in terms of paths through an individual use case.

In Chapter 4 we'll look at control flow graphs, a graph oriented approach to designing tests based on modeling paths through a use case. For use case based testing, control flow graphs have a lot going for them: easy to learn, work nicely with risk driven testing (which we'll discuss), provide a way to estimate number of needed tests, and can also be re-used for design of load tests.

Chapter 5 looks at two alternate techniques for working with use cases at this level of test: decision tables and pairwise testing.

A decision table is a table showing combinations of inputs with their associated outputs and/or actions (effects): briefly, each row of the decision table describes a separate path through the use case.

For some use cases any combination of input values (or most) is valid and describes a path through the use case. In such cases, the number of paths becomes prohibitive to describe, much less test! Chapter 5 concludes with a technique to address such use cases: pairwise testing.

21

## *PART III SINGLE SCENARIO*

In this part of the book we arrive at the 10,000-foot view and test design will focus on a single scenario of a use case.

While a scenario represents a single path through the system from a black-box perspective, at the code level different inputs to the same scenario likely cause the code to execute differently. Chapter 6 looks at test design from scenario inputs in the hope that we are more fully testing the paths through the actual code, looking at the most widely discussed topics in input testing: error guessing, random input testing, equivalence partitioning, and boundary value analysis.

For a use case scenario with more than a single input, after selecting test inputs for each separate input there's the question of how to test the inputs in combination. Chapter 6 concludes with ideas for "working smart" in striking the balance between rigor and practicality for testing inputs in combination.

Chapter 7 looks at additional (and a bit more advanced) techniques for describing inputs and how they are used to do equivalence partitioning and boundary value analysis testing. The chapter begins with a look at syntax diagrams, which will look very familiar as they re-use directed graphs (which you'll have already seen used as control flow graphs in Chapter 4).

Regular expressions are cousins of syntax diagrams, though not graphic (visual) in nature. While much has been written about regular expressions, a goal in Chapter 7 is to make a bit more specific how regular expressions relate to equivalence partitioning and boundary value analysis. A point that doesn't always seem to come across in discussing the use of regular expressions in test design.

For the adventuresome at heart the last technique discussed in Chapter 7 is recursive definitions and will include examples written in Prolog (Programming in Logic). Recursion is one of those topics that people are sometimes intimidated by. But it is truly a Swiss-army knife for defining, partitioning and doing boundary value analysis of all types of inputs (and outputs) be they numeric in nature, sets of things, Boolean or syntactic.

## PART IV OPERATIONS

In Part IV, the final part of the book, we arrive at "ground level": test design from the individual operations of a use case scenario.

A use case describes the behavior of an application or system as a sequence of steps, some of which result in the invocation of an operation in the system. The operation is the finest level of granularity for which we'll be looking at test design.

Just as varying inputs may cause execution of different code paths through a single use case scenario, other factors – e.g. violated preconditions – may cause execution of different code paths through a single operation.

In Chapter 8 Preconditions, Postconditions and Invariants: Thinking About How Operations Fail, we'll look at specifying the expected behavior of abstract data types and objects – model-based specification – and apply it to use case failure analysis: the analysis of potential ways a use case operation might fail. In doing so, the reader will learn some things about preconditions and postconditions they forgot to mention in "Use Case 101"!

You may find Chapter 8 the most challenging in the book as it involves lightweight formal methods to systematically *calculate* preconditions as a technique for failure analysis. If prior to reading this book your only exposure to preconditions and postconditions has been via the use case literature, this chapter may be a bit like, as they say, "drinking from a fire hose".  For the reader not interested in diving this deep, the chapter concludes with a section titled The Least You Need to Know About Preconditions, Postconditions and Invariants, providing *one fundamental lesson and three simple rules* that the reader can use on absolutely any use case anytime.

Having gained some insight into the true relationship between preconditions, postconditions and invariants in Chapter 8, Chapter 9 provides "lower-tech" ways to identify preconditions that could lead to the failure of an operation. We'll look at ways to use models built from sets and relations (i.e. discrete math for testers) to help spot preconditions without actually going through the formalization of *calculating* the precondition. More generally we'll find that these models are a good way to brainstorm tests for use cases at the operation level.

# PART I: USE CASE DIAGRAM

## TEST DESIGN FROM 30,000 FEET

While use case diagrams are not what Binder terms a "test-ready model"[7] they provide valuable input to the test design process helping answer questions such as:

- Faced with writing test cases for a new application: Where do I start?!
- Am I missing any use cases that I need for adequate testing?
- Are there ways to prioritize use cases, e.g. to better budget my time in test design?
- How should the use cases be tested in concert, i.e. integration tested?

In this, Part I of the book, I hope to persuade you that the use case diagram is a good place to start in answering such questions. Part I deals with the view of the application from 30,000 feet: the use case diagram. At this level the system is a set of actors, interacting with a system, described as set of use cases.

Let's start with an example use case diagram. This particular example will serve as a common thread throughout the book.

## USE CASE DIAGRAM EXAMPLE

Figure 0-1 presents a typical use case diagram for a new public library book management system. There are three key bits to the use case diagram we'll be concerning ourselves with: the "actors" (stick figures) showing classes of users of the system, the use cases (bubbles) which describe how the system will be used, and relationships between actors and use cases (lines) showing who can / is-allowed-to do what.

There are four actors presented in the use case diagram:

---

[7] Robert Binder, *Testing Object-Oriented Systems: Models, Patterns, and Tools*, 2000. See "Cartoons or Test-Ready Models?"

- Book Curator is the overall manager of the portfolio of books in the library
- Librarian serves to manage the day to day lending of books in the library
- Self Service Kiosk is not a person, but rather a new kiosk system the library is trying for select library users with special library cards. The Self Service Kiosk allows these special users to lend and return books themselves without the assistance of a librarian
- And finally, Internet User is a person that uses the available internet connection to query book availability.

The identified use cases these actors can perform are:

- Do Book Search
- Reserve Books
- Cancel Book Reservations
- Manage Book Transfers
- Lend Books
- Return Books

Use case **Reserve Books** is used to put a hold on books that are checked out; it essentially lets a reader "wait in line" for the books. **Cancel Book Reservations** removes a reader from the waiting list; e.g. if they lose interest or find the book elsewhere. Use case Manage Book Loans is used to manage the loaning of books to and from other libraries; e.g. a reader may request the library transfer a book from a branch across town to their local branch library. The purpose of the other use cases is self-evident.

Finally, lines associate actors with the use cases they can execute. Some use cases can only be executed by one actor (**Manage Book Transfers** can only be done by a curator), while other use cases can be executed by all actors (e.g. everyone can do searches for books).

Example in hand, we're ready to start test design!

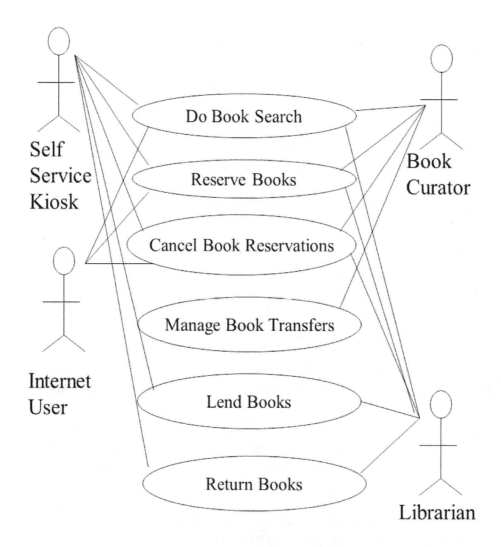

Figure 0-1 Use case diagram for library book management system

# Overview of Chapters 1, 2 and 3

As test design in Parts II-IV will be based on the use cases of our use case diagram, it makes sense to begin by asking: Is the use case diagram missing any use cases essential for adequately testing? This is addressed in Chapter 1 where we look at the use of a C.R.U.D. matrix, a tool allowing you to judge test adequacy by how well the use cases of the use case diagram cover the data life-cycle of entities in your system. Not only does the C.R.U.D. matrix test the adequacy of the use case diagram, it is essentially a high level test case for the entire system, providing expected inputs (read), and outputs (create, update, delete) for the entire system in a compact succinct form.

Still working at the use case diagram level, in Chapter 2 we look at another tool – the operational profile – as a way to help you, the tester, concentrate on the most frequently used use cases, and hence those having a greater chance of failure in the hands of the user. The chapter concludes with ways to use the operational profile, e.g. budgeting your time in test design, and in load and stress testing.

Chapter 3 wraps up our look at testing at the use case diagram level by introducing techniques for testing the use cases in concert, i.e. integration testing of the use cases.

# Chapter 1 TEST ADEQUACY OF A USE CASE DIAGRAM

The strategy we will be looking at in this book involves using a set of use cases associated with a use case diagram – the view of the system to be tested from 30,000 feet -- as a starting point for test design. As such it makes sense to first begin by asking: Is the use case diagram missing any use cases essential for adequately testing?

Originating in the 1970s as part of Structured Systems Analysis and Design, the C.R.U.D. matrix has become part of the use case tool kit. In this chapter we'll look at how the C.R.U.D. matrix is used to kick-off our test design by helping us determine the test adequacy of the use case diagram.

## TESTING ADEQUACY: VIEWING USE CASES THROUGH THE EYES OF THE DATA

The question of test adequacy – what it is, how to measure or demonstrate it -- is a much researched topic in testing[8]. As this is a book for us, the working stiffs, it will suffice to say that test adequacy is typically demonstrated via how well a suite of tests "cover" the item from which tests are being designed. This is called test coverage. Here's how ISTQB[9] defines it:

- "Test coverage is the degree  ... to which a specified coverage item has been exercised by a test suite"

While most of the techniques in this book use the use case as the basis for test coverage – How well do the tests cover some aspect of a use case? – at the use case diagram level where our test design starts, we need some ruler that both measures collections of use cases as a whole, and is separate from the use cases themselves.

---

[8] Goodenough and Gerhart's 1975 paper (*Toward a Theory of Test Data Selection*) is usually cited as a seminal paper kicking off research in the testing community on this topic.
[9] International Software Testing Qualifications Board (ISTQB), Standard glossary of terms used in Software Testing, Version 2.1, 2010

Test coverage is a form of measurement; and to measure something you need a ruler apart from the thing you are measuring.

For this we'll need to drop down out of the clouds at the 30,000-foot level (the use case diagram) down to ground level, to the data that underlies your business domain.

If one were to boil computing down to its most elemental form, it's really about affecting change on data. And of those – change and data – data is really the more fundamental: you can certainly picture data that never changes, but how can you even imagine change without there first being *something to change.*

Figure 1-1 illustrates the relationship between the use cases of a diagram, and the data of the system the use cases describe. It's a many-many relationship: many use cases can touch the same data element, and many data elements can be touched by a single use case. A use case's view of the world is a view of how it – the use case – changes data. It's a view of data and what happens to the data from the perspective of a single use case.

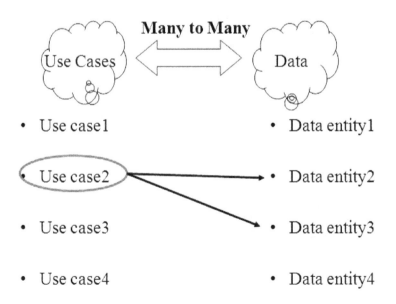

Figure 1-1 Each use case views the world of data it individually touches.

But to see what we may have missed we need to switch to the other side of Figure 1-1, the data side, and look at the world thru the eyes of each element of data asking "Which use cases touch me *collectively*"? This is illustrated in See Figure 1-2.

Looking at the system from the perspective of the data provides insights into how use cases may need to be tested in concert – use case integration testing; we'll talk about this in Chapter 2 – but additionally what data may have not been exercised adequately by the collective set of use cases in the use case diagram, for example because we may be missing a use case.

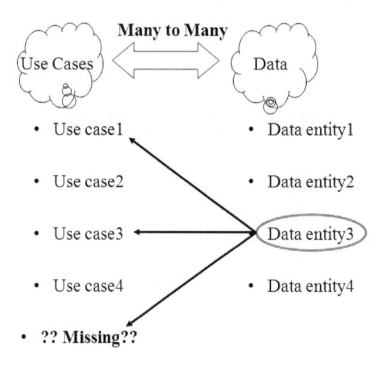

Figure 1-2 Viewing the use cases that collectively modify each data element provides a way to spot data that may not be exercised by the use case diagram as a whole.

## The C.R.U.D. Matrix

The C.R.U.D. matrix originated in the 1970s-80s as part of the structured analysis and design wave in software development. In structured analysis and design, system modeling focused on a process model – say via a dataflow diagram – and a data model, e.g. a entity-relationship diagram.[10] What was needed was a way to make sure the two jived with one another. The C.R.U.D. matrix provided this. The C.R.U.D. matrix provides a way to analyze interaction of process and data by saying all computing boils down to basically four types of interactions between process (change) and data: Creating data, Reading data, Updating existing data, or Deleting data, hence the name C.R.U.D. (Numerous alternate categorizations and extensions based on this theme have been proposed, but you get the idea).

The C.R.U.D. matrix has been thoroughly covered in the software literature primarily in terms of databases. But it's also found its way into the use case and testing community [11], [12], [13]

Specific to use case driven testing, Binder[14] has described the use of a C.R.U.D. matrix as a basis for determining test coverage as part of his Extended Use Case Test pattern. As Binder notes *"Test suites developed from individual use cases .. cannot guarantee that all of the problem domain classes in the system under test have been reached. The Covered in C.R.U.D. pattern is a simple technique for identifying such omissions"*

## From Use Case Diagram to C.R.U.D. Matrix

Returning to our use case diagram from Figure 0-1 let's look at how we can build a C.R.U.D. matrix to help determine the test adequacy of the use case of the diagram.

---

[10] Peter Chen, *Entity-Relationship Modeling: Historical Events, Future Trends, and Lessons Learned* is a great white-paper read on the history of the ERD. While we take it as a de facto standard now, that was not so when it first came out!
[11] Armour and Miller, *Advanced Use Case Modeling*, 2001
[12] Karl Wiegers, *Software Requirements*, second edition, 2003
[13] Martin Pol et.al., *Software Testing, A Guide to the TMap Approach*, 2001
[14] Robert Binder, *Testing Object-Oriented Systems: Models, Patterns, and Tools*, 2000

A note on terminology before we start. There's no set standard on how a C.R.U.D. matrix is drawn. You may look at three authors and see three variations, e.g. what's on the X-axis of one may be the Y-axis of another. But the idea is always the same: we use a matrix to express the relation between computation – operations, process, tasks, use cases – and data – class, object, entity, record, etc.

## ROWS AND COLUMNS OF THE MATRIX

We begin by simply listing the use cases of our use case diagram as rows of the C.R.U.D. matrix as in Figure 1-3. In addition to the use cases, you may find it useful to add one extra row at the bottom, and label it something like "Don't Care"; As we start working through the C.R.U.D. matrix we may find some aspect of the data that isn't being exercised (that's the whole point of the C.R.U.D. matrix). But it also may be that in some cases we determine it's ok, and will consider that out of scope for test design. This row – Don't Care – allows us to make a note of that fact.

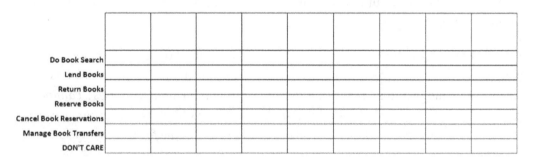

Figure 1-3 Use cases of the use case diagram are listed as rows in the matrix.

Next, as columns of the matrix we list the data entities pertinent to the testing of the system. Data entities are those things in your business, real or abstract, for which the system will be tracking information.

I'm using the term "data entity" to be general and avoid implementation specific terms like "object", "class" or "database table". That's not to say these things are excluded from what a tester might use in the C.R.U.D. matrix; I'm just trying to avoid giving the impression that the C.R.U.D. matrix is *only* relevant to testers working e.g. on object-oriented systems, or database systems where object / data models are available for the tester to reference.

In use case development, this process of "discovering" the data entities relevant to the use cases is called domain analysis.[15] And as a tester one may have to do a bit of domain analysis. Just remember, as a tester, you aren't doing domain analysis in order to arrive at an object-model or data-model that will influence the architecture of your system (let the system analysts and developers lose sleep over that!). You just need a set of data entities as basis for judging the test adequacy of the use cases, i.e. how well do they exercise the underlying data. So relax and dig in.

| | Titles | Copies of Books | Check Out Requests | Reservation Requests | Branch Library Transfers | Borrowers | Librarians | Curators | Branch Libraries |
|---|---|---|---|---|---|---|---|---|---|
| Do Book Search | | | | | | | | | |
| Lend Books | | | | | | | | | |
| Return Books | | | | | | | | | |
| Reserve Books | | | | | | | | | |
| Cancel Book Reservations | | | | | | | | | |
| Manage Book Transfers | | | | | | | | | |
| DON'T CARE | | | | | | | | | |

Figure 1-4 We list the data entities pertinent to the testing of the system as columns of the matrix

Figure 1-4 shows our example C.R.U.D. matrix, with columns populated with data entities that seem pertinent to the test of the system. Titles is the set of book titles which the library system tracks. Copies of Books are the actual physical copies of each book title the library owns; the library may have zero copies of a particular title. Information common to all copies of a book – e.g. ISBN – are tracked with the title, rather than with each individual copy of the book. Information specific to a physical book – e.g. date acquired – is stored with each copy of the book.

Check Out Requests are the records of books checked out by library patrons. Reservation Requests are the records of patrons that are waiting for a copy of a book, for example when all copies of a title are checked out. The rest of our data entities correspond to the actors in our use case diagram: Borrowers (library patrons), Librarians, Curators, Branch Libraries.

---

[15] Armour and Miller, *Advanced Use Case Modeling*, provide good guidance on domain analysis in use case driven development.

With rows (use cases) and columns (data entities) in place, we now work through the matrix noting how each use case interacts with the data entities. The completed C.R.U.D. matrix for our library use case diagram is shown in Figure 1-5.

*An important point* to make here that will not be immediately obvious from simply *looking* at the matrix is that the act of actually working through the matrix is part of the true benefit.

By systematically analyzing every use case in terms of each data entity, and asking "Does it create, read, update or delete this?", you are doing test design. Think of the C.R.U.D. matrix as a high level test case for the entire system, providing expected inputs (read), and outputs (create, update, delete) for the entire system in a compact, succinct form.

A very important part of working through the C.R.U.D. matrix –beyond testing the adequacy of the use case diagram -- is the discovery and "Ah, Ha!" moments that will occur while systematically analyzing the interaction of use cases and data entities. As a test designer, be prepared to capture ideas, issues, assumptions, notes and questions that will inevitably arise as you work through the C.R.U.D..

Working through the C.R.U.D. matrix is test design!

| | Titles | Copies of Books | Check Out Requests | Reservation Requests | Branch Library Transfers | Borrowers | Librarians | Curators | Branch Libraries |
|---|---|---|---|---|---|---|---|---|---|
| Do Book Search | R | R | R | R | R | R | R | R | |
| Lend Books | R | R | R, C | R, U | R | R | R | | |
| Return Books | R | R | R, U | R, U | | R | R | | |
| Reserve Books | R | R | R | C | | R | R | R | |
| Cancel Book Reservations | R | R | | U | | R | R | R | |
| Manage Book Transfers | R | R | R | R | R, C, U | | | R | R |
| DON'T CARE | | | | | | | | | |

Figure 1-5 Working through the C.R.U.D. matrix is test design, providing expected inputs (reads) and outputs (create, update, delete) for the entire system in a succinct format

## Use Case Descriptions via the C.R.U.D. Matrix

Let's walk through the matrix of Figure 1-5 row by row looking at the interaction of use cases with data. In the textual use case descriptions that follow, their interaction with data entities (columns of the matrix) are categorized parenthetically with create, read, update, or delete.

- **Do Book Search** - This use case allows authenticated librarians, book curators and borrowers (self service kiosk or internet user) to search for books. It pulls information (read) from book titles (e.g. publisher, ISBN), and the status of each particular copy of a book in terms of whether it is checked-out, reserved or on loan to a branch library.

- **Lend Books** - This use case describes the lending of a book or books. It assumes a physical copy of a book is in hand, i.e. either a borrower walks the book up to a librarian or self-service kiosk (equipped with a scanner) for checkout. The use case validates the borrower (read), and/or ensures the librarian is logged-in (read). As a sanity check the use case confirms that this copy of the book is not showing as being checked out (read), reserved by someone other than the borrower (read), or being on loan to a branch library (read), any of which would indicate a problem with tracking. If all looks valid, a new record tracking this check-out of this book is created. If the book was reserved by the borrower on-line and they are now picking it up, the reservation request is updated as having been fulfilled (update).

- **Return Books** - This use case describes the return of a checked out book. As with the lending use case, it assumes a physical copy of a book is in hand, i.e. either a borrower walks the book up to a librarian or self-service kiosk for check-in. The use case confirms that this copy of the book is checked out to the authenticated borrower (read) and if being dropped off to a librarian (not kiosk) that the librarian is logged-in (read). The previously created check out request is updated to show the book has been returned (update). In addition, a check is made of pending reservation requests for this book (read); if one exists (next in line for the book if there are multiple), the reservation is flagged to notify person reserving the book (update).

- **Reserve Books** - Sometimes a borrower is interested in a book, but all copies are check out. Alternatively, because books can only be checked out at a self service kiosk or by a librarian, both physically located at the library, an internet user may choose to reserve a book until able to get to the library. Curators too may need to reserve a book, e.g. to pull it temporarily out of circulation. This use case addresses these situations. Borrower, curator and/or librarian (if reservation is done through librarian) are authenticated (read). Title is validated (read), and a check is made that copies of the book are actually owned by the library (read), i.e. the library may have a book title, but no physical copies, in which case a reservation cannot be made. A check is also made as to whether all copies are lent, or if some are available for immediate pickup (read). If all is good, a reservation request is created for a copy of the book (create).

- **Cancel Book Reservations** - If a borrower has reserved a book, but later decides the book is not wanted, the reservation can be cancelled. Alternatively, either curators or librarians may need to cancel reservations for some reason. This use case covers these situations. Borrower, curator and/or librarian are authenticated (read), then the reservation request cancelled (update).
- **Manage Book Transfers** - Books are sometimes temporarily or permanently swapped between libraries by library curators. This use case describes that process. The curator and branch library the books are going to, or coming from, are authenticated (read).  Checks are made that the books to be transferred are not checked out (read), reserved (read), or part of other active transfer requests (read).  If everything checks out, a new transfer request is created, or an existing request may be updated.

## WHAT'S MISSING?

With C.R.U.D. matrix completed, we can now ask: How adequately does our set of use cases – our basis of testing -- exercise the full life-cycle of the data entities we've identified? We check this with our C.R.U.D. matrix by scanning each data entity's column looking for the presence of a "C", "R", "U", and "D", indicating that the data's life-cycle has been fully exercised by the set of use cases.

In doing this we note the following holes in our coverage of the data:

- **Titles** is read by every use case, but none create, update or delete a title.

- **Copies of Books** is read by all use cases, but none create, update or delete a copy of a book.
- **Check Out Requests** and **Branch Library Transfers** are created, read and updated by our use cases, but no use case deletes a check out request or library transfer.
- **Borrowers**, **Librarians**, **Curators** and **Branch Libraries** are all read by our use cases, but none create, update or delete these data entities.

To beef up coverage of the data, we decide to we'll need two new use cases, shown in the updated C.R.U.D. matrix of Figure 1-6.

- **Add Books to Library Database** - This use case adds a new copy of a book to the library holdings. But before it can add a new copy, the title is validated (read) to make sure its registered with the library. If not, a new title record is created tracking information common to future copies of this book (create). Also, the curator making the addition is authenticated (read). Finally, a check is made of pending reservation requests for this book title (read); if one exists (next in line for the book if there are multiple), the reservation is flagged to notify person reserving the book (update).
- **Remove Books from Library Database** - This use cases removes a *copy* (but not the title) of a book from the library's holdings. The curator doing the remove is authenticated (read), the title is validated (read), the particular copy of the book to be removed is validated (read). Also, confirmation is made that the book is not currently checked out (read); not on loan to a branch library (read); and not a copy that has been pulled by a librarian for pending pickup by a borrower, e.g. was reserved on-line (read). Once validated, the tracking records for this book copy is deleted from the library tracking system, i.e. information about the particular copy, checkout history, branch library transfer history.

With these additional use cases, we still have a few holes in our coverage of the data:

- No use cases update or delete titles
- No use cases update the information kept for particular copies of each book, say to correct the date of acquisition, or from where it was acquired, etc.

- While book reservations are created, read and updated by the use cases, none delete the backlog of old reservations.
- And no use cases create, update or delete the system's borrowers, librarians, curators, or branch libraries.

To complete the C.R.U.D. matrix, we fill-in the last row ("Don't Care") to designate the data operations we are willing to allow to fall out of scope for test at this point, because say the code to support those operations is pending, or those operations are considered low risk for the time being.

It's worth emphasizing, sometimes saying what you are *not* going to test is every bit as important as saying what you are going to test ("What, you didn't test that? Had I known that I would have said something in the review of the test plan!!"). So while not common on a C.R.U.D. matrix, adding a row called "Don't Care" is a smart thing to do as a test designer.

Figure 1-6 shows the completed C.R.U.D. matrix, each column having at least one create, read, update or delete. Figure 1-7 is the corresponding updated use case diagram.

| | Titles | Copies of Books | Check Out Requests | Reservation Requests | Branch Library Transfers | Borrowers | Librarians | Curators | Branch Libraries |
|---|---|---|---|---|---|---|---|---|---|
| **Add Books to Library Database** | R, C | C | | U | | | | R | |
| **Remove Books from Library Database** | R | R, D | R, D | R | R, D | | | | |
| **Do Book Search** | R | R | R | R | R | R | R | R | |
| **Lend Books** | R | R | R, C | R, U | R | R | R | | |
| **Return Books** | R | R | R, U | R, U | | R | R | | |
| **Reserve Books** | R | R | R | C | | R | R | R | |
| **Cancel Book Reservations** | R | R | | U | | R | R | R | |
| **Manage Book Transfers** | R | R | R | R | R, C, U | | | R | R |
| **DON'T CARE** | U, D | U | | D | | C, U, D | C,U,D | C,U,D | C,U,D |

Figure 1-6 Updated C.R.U.D. matrix with two new use cases (first two rows, highlighted). The last row "Don't Care" shows data operations we are allowing to fall out of scope for testing

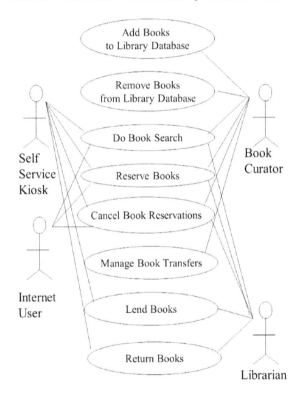

Figure 1-7 Updated Use Case Diagram corresponding to C.R.U.D. matrix of Figure 1-6

## CHAPTER REVIEW

Let's review what we've covered in this chapter.

A use case diagram – the view of the system to be tested from 30,000 feet – is a great starting point for test design. As such it makes sense to begin by asking: Is the use case diagram missing any use cases essential for adequately testing? For this a C.R.U.D. matrix is a great tool, allowing you to judge test adequacy by how well the use cases cover the data life-cycle of entities in your system.

Not only does the C.R.U.D. matrix test the adequacy of the use case diagram, it is essentially a high level test case for the entire system, providing expected inputs (read), and outputs (create, update, delete) for the entire system in a compact succinct form.

An important part of working through the C.R.U.D. matrix is the "Ah, Ha!" moments that will occur while systematically analyzing the interaction of use cases and data entities, providing valuable testing insights.

While not common on a C.R.U.D. matrix, adding a row call "Don't Care" let's you as a tester state explicitly what you are seeing as out of scope for test. Saying what you are *not* testing can sometimes be just as important as saying what you are going to test.

# Chapter 2 FROM USE CASE DIAGRAM TO OPERATIONAL PROFILE

In the last chapter we looked at the use of a C.R.U.D. matrix to evaluate the test adequacy of the use cases associated with a use case diagram. Now we're ready to dive deep and start designing tests from the use cases, right? *Well, maybe.* First however ask: Does it really make sense to spend the same amount of time and rigor on test design for each use case?

A use case with many bugs can seem reliable if the user spends so little time running it that none of the many bugs are found. Conversely, a use case that has few bugs can seem unreliable if the user spends so much time running it that all those few bugs are found. This is the concept of perceived reliability: it is the reliability the user experiences, as opposed to a reliability measure in terms of, say, defect density.

An operational profile is a tool used in software reliability engineering to spot the high traffic paths through your system. This allows you, the test designer, to concentrate on the most frequently used use cases, and hence those having a greater chance of failure in the hands of the user. By taking such an approach, you work smarter—not harder—to deliver a reliable product.

## FINDING THE HIGH TRAFFIC USE CASES IN YOUR SYSTEM

The field of software reliability engineering (SRE) is about increasing customer satisfaction by delivering a reliable product while minimizing engineering costs. Use case-driven development and SRE are a natural match, both being usage-driven styles of product development. What SRE adds to use case-driven development is a discipline for focusing time, effort, and resources on use cases in proportion to their estimated frequency of use[16] to *maximize quality while minimizing development costs.* Or as John Musa says, "More reliable software, faster and cheaper."

---

[16] In addition to frequency of use, criticality is also an important factor in determining which use cases require added attention. We'll address that later in this chapter.

A key concept in SRE is quantifying frequency of product use by the user. Use cases already provide a discrete unit for describing product use; SRE provides the means to quantify that use with what is called an operational profile.

Figure 2-1 and Figure 2-2 show an operational profile in the form of a table and Pareto chart (respectively) for the updated public library book management system use case diagram from the previous chapter, repeated here in Figure 2-3 for convenience. In Figure 2-1 the second column shows the estimated number of times daily a use case will be executed; the third column shows the relative frequency of each use case, i.e. how frequently a use case is used relative to the others.

In Figure 2-2 the left scale of the Y-axis displays the estimated number of times per day we expect each use case to be executed; the right scale of the Y-axis the cumulative relative frequency (which sums to 100%). Notice that over *90% of the usage* is accounted for by just three use cases: **Do Book Search**, **Lend Books**, and **Return Books**.

| Use Case | Est. Times Executed Daily | Relative Frequency |
|---|---|---|
| Do Book Search | 2110 | 44% |
| Lend Books | 1100 | 23% |
| Return Books | 1100 | 23% |
| Reserve Books | 211 | 4% |
| Cancel Book Reservations | 211 | 4% |
| Manage Book Transfers | 20 | 0.421% |
| Add Books to Library Database | 0.5 | 0.011% |
| Remove Books from Library Database | 0.05 | 0.001% |

Figure 2-1 Operational profile (table) for use case diagram of Figure 2-3

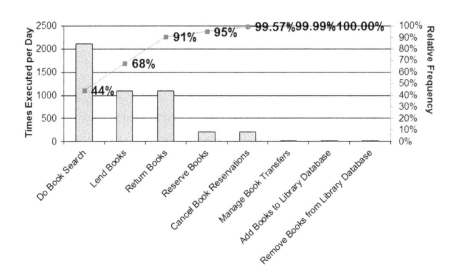

**Estimated Daily Execution of each Use Cases**

Figure 2-2 Operational profile (Pareto chart) for use case diagram of Figure 2-3

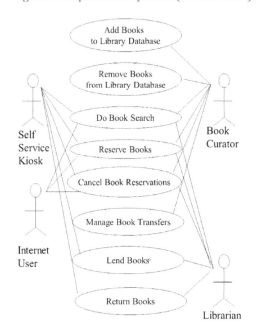

Figure 2-3 Use case diagram for library book management system

43

Now, looking at Figure 2-1 and Figure 2-2, ask yourself this: Is applying the same amount of time and effort in test design to all use cases really the best strategy? Another way to look at the frequency of use information of use cases is in terms of opportunities for failure. Think of it like this: use case **Do Book Search** is not just executed 2000+ a day; rather it has *2000+ opportunities for failure a day*. Each time a use case is executed by a user it is an opportunity for the user to stumble onto a latent defect in the code; to discover a missed requirement; to discover just how user un-friendly the interface really is; to tax the performance of critical computing resources of the system like memory, disk and CPU. With each additional execution of a use case the probability goes up that the execution will result in failure. Viewed as opportunities for failure in your production system, doesn't it make sense to design and execute tests in relative proportion to the opportunities for failure that each use case will receive in production?

Assuming your convinced it's worth doing a bit of analysis into which use cases are most highly trafficked before diving into writing tests ( "I just blew my budgeted time for test design writing tests for use cases that are rarely used!"), the next step is, how do we build an operational profile from the use case diagram? Let's tackle that next.[17]

## THE QFD MATRIX

QFD (Quality Function Deployment) is a product-planning tool that is used to translate business drivers into the technical requirements and design aspects of a product. Though originally developed for manufacturing industries in the 1960s, today QFD-like ideas are being used successfully for all sorts of applications, including software development, the services industry, and process management, and is considered an essential part of the quality improvement toolkit.

---

[17] If empirical data is available, e.g. web portal statistics from an existing system, that can also be used for an operational profile.

QFD boiled down to simple mechanics is about establishing priorities, the key tool being a QFD matrix. QFD is an ideal tool for representing a use case diagram – establishing links between actors and use cases -- and for generating an operational profile from that diagram.[18]

The easiest way to see how to generate an operational profile from a use case diagram using a QFD matrix is with an example. Using the use case diagram from Figure 2-3 as our starting point, we build a simple QFD matrix, here implemented as an Excel spreadsheet (see Figure 2-4 ). In this matrix, all actors of the use case diagram are placed in rows, and the use cases are placed across the top as columns.

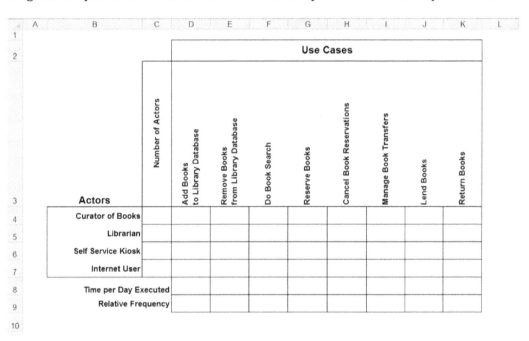

Figure 2-4 QFD matrix for use case diagram of Figure 2-3. Rows of matrix are actors from the use case diagram; columns are the use cases.

------------------------------------------------

[18] You really don't need to know much more about QFD to build a use case diagram, but if you want to learn more refer to Denney, *Succeeding with Use Cases, Part 1*, which gives a broader treatment of the combined use of QFD with use cases.

*QUANTIFY NUMBERS OF ACTORS IN USE CASE DIAGRAM*

The next step in analyzing your use case traffic is to quantify the number of each type of actor in the use case diagram. How many book curators are there? How about librarians; self-service kiosks? Don't get hung-up on precise numbers; ball park numbers are all you need to understand the relative numbers of actors, e.g. how many librarians do you have relative to curators: Same amount; twice as many? How about internet users; how many more than kiosks: Twice as many; a hundred times as many?

At this point you might say, "*I have no idea how many internet users to expect!*". To which I would respond: Bingo, we've just identified a non-functional requirement that needs clarification! Asking questions about numbers of actors in the use case diagram is a healthy thing to be doing early on.

Keeping in mind that the goal is to get ballpark numbers for the operational profile you might try this. Rather than agonizing over whether there is one versus two book curators, or fifty versus two hundred internet users, try working with *orders of magnitude*. An order of magnitude estimate is one given in terms of a factor of 10:

$10^0 = 1$

$10^1 = 10$

$10^2 = 100$

$10^3 = 1000$

$10^4 = 10,000$

etc..

By their nature of separation, it's usually easier to come up with orders of magnitude estimates. What's the *average* life of a person? Rather than getting into debates about the numerous factors that affect people's longevity—health, lifestyle, country, even what century—it's pretty clear that it's on an order of magnitude of 100 years; 10 is way too small and 1000 is way too big. Use order of magnitude estimates to get you in the ball park, then step back and refine your estimates if you feel so inclined, doubling here, and halving there.

So for our library use case diagram you determine that as a rule of thumb, using orders of magnitude estimates there is one curator, ten librarians, one self service kiosk, and one hundred internet users that might be accessing the system each day. This information is placed in the matrix in column Number of Actors (see Figure 2-5 ).

| | Actors | Number of Actors | Add Books to Library Database | Remove Books from Library Database | Do Book Search | Reserve Books | Cancel Book Reservations | Manage Book Transfers | Lend Books | Return Books |
|---|---|---|---|---|---|---|---|---|---|---|
| | | | | | | Use Cases | | | | |
| | Curator of Books | 1 | | | | | | | | |
| | Librarian | 10 | | | | | | | | |
| | Self Service Kiosk | 1 | | | | | | | | |
| | Internet User | 100 | | | | | | | | |
| | Time per Day Executed | | | | | | | | | |
| | Relative Frequency | | | | | | | | | |

Figure 2-5 Numbers of each type of actor are entered into the matrix

## QUANTIFY USE CASE FREQUENCY OF USE BY ACTORS

With estimates of numbers of each type of actor identified you now turn to the question of who does what, i.e. which actors use what use cases .. *and how often!* In a use case diagram this information is captured as relationships – depicted as lines – between actors and use cases (Figure 2-3). In the QFD matrix it is captured by placing a number in the cell that corresponds to the intersection of an actor (row) and use case (column). The number you place in the cell is the number of times a "typical" actor of that type will execute that use case per some unit of time, say daily. If an actor never uses a particular use case the cell is left blank.

Again, using orders of magnitude to estimate frequency of use will help avoid analysis paralysis. Once in the ballpark you can step back and tweak the estimate, doubling here and halving there if you are so compelled. For the library use case diagram, orders of magnitude estimates for each actor are provided in Figure 2-6; frequency is given in times per day each use case is executed by *each* actor of that type.

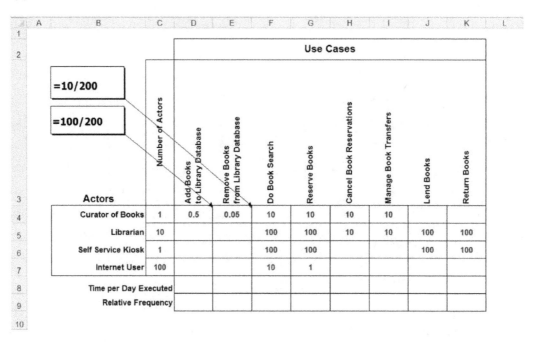

| Actors | Number of Actors | Add Books to Library Database | Remove Books from Library Database | Do Book Search | Reserve Books | Cancel Book Reservations | Manage Book Transfers | Lend Books | Return Books |
|---|---|---|---|---|---|---|---|---|---|
| Curator of Books | 1 | 0.5 | 0.05 | 10 | 10 | 10 | 10 | | |
| Librarian | 10 | | | 100 | 100 | 10 | 10 | 100 | 100 |
| Self Service Kiosk | 1 | | | 100 | 100 | | | 100 | 100 |
| Internet User | 100 | | | 10 | 1 | | | | |
| Time per Day Executed | | | | | | | | | |
| Relative Frequency | | | | | | | | | |

(Boxes: =10/200, =100/200)

Figure 2-6 Frequency of execution of each use case by actor type is entered into the matrix

Notice that the Book Curator executes the **Add Books to Library Database** use case and **Remove Books from Library Database** use case .5 and .05 times a day, respectively. Are those order of magnitude estimates? Yes; when a use case is used less than once per unit of time – here daily – you can get the order of magnitude estimate as follows.

The curator adds about 100 books (order of magnitude) a year; a year is about 200 working days, so the formula for calculating daily use is:

100 / 200 = .5

Similarly, the curator removes about 10 books a year (order of magnitude; the library is growing!), so the formula for calculating daily use is:

10 / 200 = .05

Getting estimates of the number of actors of each type and frequency of use information is the hard part of analyzing the traffic through your use cases. All that is left is to crank out the results. Figure 2-7 shows the final results: an estimate of the frequency of daily execution of each use case by all actors in the library book management system (also shown are the formulas you need for this; the top formula calculates absolute number of times per day; the bottom formula calculates relative frequency.[19])

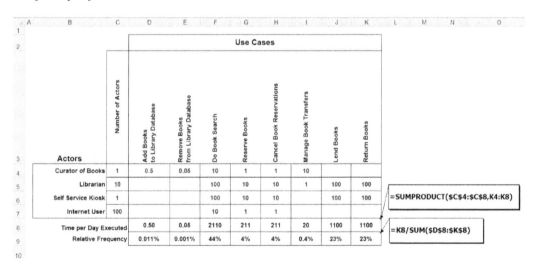

Figure 2-7 Completed QFD matrix providing frequency of use for each use case

---

[19] Formulas shown for Microsoft Excel. Your favorite spreadsheet will provide equivalent functionality.

In our QFD matrix, the rows labeled "Times per day Executed" and "Relative Frequency" correspond to the columns and axis of the same name in Figure 2-1 and Figure 2-2. In the next section we'll look at how to put these relative frequencies to work in test design.

## USING THE OPERATIONAL PROFILE IN TEST PLANNING AND DESIGN

To this point the chapter has focused on motivating the importance of operational profiles and how to use a QFD matrix to derive one from a use case diagram. Now we get to the *working smarter* part of operational profiles: putting them to work.

### TIMEBOXING: BUDGETING TEST DESIGN TIME
The strategy for test design presented is this book is to budget test design time for each use case based on an operational profile: an analysis of the frequency of use of each use case. After all, frequency of use is opportunity for failure: the more use, the more opportunities for the user to find defects.

The idea of budgeting a fixed time for some task is called timeboxing. Timeboxing is a planning strategy often associated with iterative software development in which the duration of a task (design tests for a use case) is fixed, forcing hard decisions to be made about what scope (number and rigor of tests) can be delivered in the allotted time. What's new with the approach here is that budgeted times are based on an operational profile.

To illustrate, say you've been given a week to write test cases from the use cases of the library system. During that week you estimate your team will be able to spend about 40 staff hours. To get an idea of how best to budget the teams' time, you construct a quick spreadsheet using the relative frequencies from the operational profile. Results are shown in Figure 2-8; hours budgeted (right column) have been rounded to the nearest whole hour.

| Use Case | Relative Frequency | Hours to Spend Writing Tests |
|---|---|---|
| Do Book Search | 44% | 18 |
| Lend Books | 23% | 9 |
| Return Books | 23% | 9 |
| Reserve Books | 4% | 2 |
| Cancel Book Reservations | 4% | 2 |
| Manage Book Transfers | 0.4% | 0 |
| Add Books to Library Database | 0.011% | 0 |
| Remove Books from Library Database | 0.001% | 0 |

Figure 2-8 Allocating 40 hours of test design based on the operational profile

The first thing you will notice in this example is that some tests have been allocated zero hours of test design; that is based on the low frequency of use. And this is a good time to reiterate one of the reasons use cases have gained attention in testing: in a pinch (you've run out of time for test design), the use cases you *didn't* get around to design tests for are workable substitutes for full-fledged test cases.

Alternatively you may decide you really want some tests designed for each use case regardless of how little they are used. Figure 2-9 illustrates budgeting the 40 hours of test design to strike a balance between the spirit of the operational profile and yet having some time for test design for all use cases. And I think it is the spirit of what the operational profile is showing us that is important for planning. That combined with some common sense will lead to a better allocation of time.

| Use Case | Relative Frequency | Hours to Spend Writing Tests |
|---|---|---|
| Do Book Search | 44% | 17 |
| Lend Books | 23% | 8 |
| Return Books | 23% | 8 |
| Reserve Books | 4% | 2 |
| Cancel Book Reservations | 4% | 2 |
| Manage Book Transfers | 0.4% | 1 |
| Add Books to Library Database | 0.011% | 1 |
| Remove Books from Library Database | 0.001% | 1 |

Figure 2-9 Reallocation of 40 hours honoring the spirit of the operational profile, yet still making sure each use case has at least a minimal amount of test design.

**Timeboxing, Use Case Levels of Test, and Test Rigor**

Referring back to Figure 0-3 and Figure 0-4 illustrating our strategy for test design, once budgeted time is in place for each use case (level 1), test design would proceed use case by use case, working top-down from level 2 (use case), to level 3 (single scenario) to level 4 (operations) until the budgeted time for a use case is up.

For use cases for which many hours have been budgeted, this strategy will produce tests at all levels, 2-4. And at any given level, when the option is available to increase or decrease rigor, rigor could be increased.[20] Tests at more, deeper levels, with increased rigor, will translate to more tests, with greater detail, and ultimately more test execution time for frequently used use cases.

For use cases for which few hours have been budgeted, test design may not progress deeper than level 2 (use case) or 3 (single scenario) before time is up. And at any

---

[20] For an example of what I mean by increased or decreased test design rigor, skip ahead to Chapter 4, Control Flow Graphs: Adjusting the Rigor of Test Design. Similar ideas for adjusting rigor are provided at all use case levels of test.

given level, less rigor is likely in order to accommodate for less budgeted time. Tests at fewer levels with less rigor will translate to fewer, coarser granularity tests for use cases used infrequently.

## RISK EXPOSURE AND CRITICAL USE CASES

Sometimes frequency of use alone doesn't fully account for the reliability required of a use case. Take for example an air bag in your car. The level of reliability we require from an air-bag is not in proportion to its frequency of use; it is seldom if ever used, and if used, used only once. But you really hope it has been thoroughly tested. To address these situations, in this section we'll look at an extension to the operational profile to analyze the *risk exposure* of use cases.

First off, what do we mean by "risk"? The type of risk we'll be talking about is quantified, and used for example in talking about the reliability of safety critical systems. It's also the type of "risk" that the actuarial scientists use in thinking about financial risks: for example the financial risk an insurance company runs when they issue flood insurance in a given geographical area.

In this type of risk, the *risk of an event* is defined as the *likelihood* that the event will actually happen, multiplied by the expected *severity* of the event. If you have an event that is catastrophic in impact, but rarely happens, it could be low risk (dying from shock as a result of winning the lottery for example).

What's all this about "events"; what does that have to do with use cases? Well, each time your customer runs a use case, there is some chance that they will encounter a defect in the product. That's an event. So what you'd like to have is a way to quantify the relative risk of such events from use case to use case so you can work smarter, planning to spend time making the riskier use cases more reliable. The way we do this is risk exposure. Likelihood is expressed in terms of frequency or a probability. The product – likelihood times severity – is the *risk exposure.*

| Use Case | Frequency * Number of Oppportunities for Failure Daily | Severity = $$ to Resolve Problem (Order of Magnitude) | Risk Risk Exposure ($$ per Day) | % of Total Risk Exposure |
|---|---|---|---|---|
| Arrange Payment | 355 | $ 10 | $ 3,550 | 3% |
| Place Nat'l Order | 350 | $ 100 | $ 35,000 | 25% |
| Enter Customer Data | 340 | $ 100 | $ 34,000 | 24% |
| Order Product | 340 | $ 100 | $ 34,000 | 24% |
| Request Catalog | 129 | $ 10 | $ 1,290 | 1% |
| Check Order Status | 100 | $ 10 | $ 1,000 | 1% |
| Place Local Order | 50 | $ 100 | $ 5,000 | 4% |
| Place Int'l Order | 25 | $ 1,000 | $ 25,000 | 18% |
| Cancel Order | 25 | $ 100 | $ 2,500 | 2% |
| TOTAL | 1714 | TOTAL | $ 141,340 | 100% |

Figure 2-10 Calculating the Risk Exposure of Use Cases

Figure 2-10 illustrates extending an operational profile for a sales order system to calculate risk exposure. Let's walk through the example.

## Frequency

The first two columns are just like those from the operational profile of Figure 2-1. The first is simply the use case, the second the estimated times daily the use case is executed. But rather than saying that use case Arrange Payment is executed 355 times a day, think of it like this: use case Arrange Payment has 355 opportunities a day to fail. And Request Catalog has 129 opportunities a day to fail. It's the same concept we've seen in the operational profile of Figure 2-1, just restated in such a way to emphasize how it fits into the overall calculation of risk

## Severity

The third column estimates the severity of correcting a failure. The severity of a use case failure may be hard to pin down quantitatively. Here are some factors to consider. First, there is the matter of the unit of measure for severity. Common units of measure for severity are cost, lost time (e.g. system downtime), and for safety-critical systems, deaths and/or injuries. Given any one of these units of measure – cost, lost time, etc.. – you have to also decide what it is that needs to be measured. For example for cost, is it the cost to repair a failure; or the cost of lost revenue due to a failure; perhaps both?

Use caution in arbitrarily adopting a scale of say, 1=low severity, 2=medium severity, 3=high severity. Remember, the resulting profile will be used to allocate time, effort and resources: if you plan on ranking one use case three times more severe as another, make sure it truly is three times more severe in some absolute sense.

Next, as Musa et al.[21] point out, the severity of failure depends a lot on whose perspective you choose to measure it from. A defect that is relatively inexpensive to correct from a development standpoint can be catastrophic to a customer, and vice versa.

Finally there is the issue of actually putting a number to the severity. Keep in mind the goal is to get relative values for a profile. So rather than agonizing over whether the severity of the defect represents 5 vs. 6 hours of down-time, consider Musa et al.'s suggestion to round-off severity estimates to the nearest order of magnitude.

Considering all these factors, for the sales order system example of Figure 2-10 the unit of measure selected is an order of magnitude estimate of dollars to correct problems for the customer once discovered. The reasoning for estimates of severity for this example might go something like the following.

Use cases such as Arrange Payment, Request Catalog, and Check Order Status can typically be fixed on-line by a customer representative and are estimated at an order of magnitude of ten dollars to correct. For example, customer orders catalog, system fails to issue request for catalog and customer never gets it. Customer phones and complains and the problem is fixed with the re-issue of a catalog. Pretty straightforward.

---

[21] John Musa, Anthony Iannino, and Kazuhira Okumoto, Software Reliability: Measurement, Prediction, Application. McGraw-Hill, 1990

One might decide, however, that use cases that involve the shipment of goods within the country – Place Local Order and Place National Order -- are more on the order of magnitude of one hundred dollars to fix. For example, customer orders widget A, but system issues request for widget B. Customer gets wrong widget and phones to complain. Fixing this involves cost of labor, shipping, and insurance to have wrong widget picked up from customer, shipped back to the warehouse, and re-stocked.

Similarly problems with international orders might be even more expensive to fix. They incur the same types of costs to fix as local and national orders – only more expensive – plus tariffs going and coming, etc.. Use case Place International Order one might estimate at on an order of magnitude of a thousand dollars to fix. And so on.

## Risk

Risk exposure in the fourth column is the product of the frequency and severity. Risk exposure represents the risk in dollars to run a use case. It doesn't mean that is how much money you are necessarily losing; it is the potential loss you are exposed to – hence the term *risk exposure* -- from running a use case. It's just a way to compare the risk of one use case to another.

Column five then calculates the overall percent of total risk exposure each use case represents. This last column can be used for timeboxing test design time as described in the last section, Timeboxing: Budgeting Test Design Time.

## Concluding Thoughts

Adding information about the criticality of use cases to your operational profile will of course require more effort. Deciding whether or not it's worth it depends on a number of things.

If your business has elements that are safety-critical, mission-critical, business-critical, etc.. you probably already spend time thinking about how things fail and the cost of failures, so extending the operational profile is probably not that big a jump for you.

On the other hand, even if you deal in critical systems, if the cost of all your failures is astronomical, or if the cost of all your failures are on the same order of magnitude, including severity in the profile might not buy you that much; profiling by frequency of use might be all you need.

And for some businesses, making the connection between things that fail and their associated cost may be hard to establish with much certainty. In the end it really comes down to asking: "What do I have to lose when a use case fails, can I quantify it and will that help me in planning?"

## RISK EXPOSURE AND DATA

It is sometimes useful for test planning to understand the risk of a release – as represented by a set of use cases – in terms of the data; e.g. what data has a high risk of being corrupted, and hence warrants closer scrutiny in testing. Looking forward in the book, this will be a good thing to know for prioritizing data lifecycle testing (Chapter 3), and again when we look at ways to brainstorm tests based on relations in the data (Chapter 9 ). So let' look at a quick way to leverage the work we've already done in terms of the operational profile and C.R.U.D. matrix to help us spot high risk data in our system.

In the previous section we looked at extending the operational profile to analyze the risk exposure of use cases. We now look the use of the operational profile to analyze the risk exposure of the underlying data of your system.

The two things we need for analyzing risk exposure is expected frequency of an event, and severity of the event. The operational profile of our use cases provides us with the expected frequency; and the C.R.U.D. matrix provides a way to gauge the severity that each use case poses to the data. Here's a way to put the two together to provide the risk exposure of the system's underlying data.

Figure 2-11 is another simple QFD matrix. Remember, QFD was introduced earlier in the chapter as a tool for building an operational profile. It's common in QFD to link the output from one matrix to the inputs of another. In Figure 2-11 we've taken the output from the matrix of Figure 2-7 (the relative frequency of each use case; bottom row) and used it as the input to our new matrix for computing data risk exposure (Figure 2-11, column Relative Frequency). As columns of the new QFD matrix we list the data entities from the C.R.U.D. matrix of Figure 1-6; this is the data for which we wish to find the risk exposure.

All that remains is to express the relative severity each use case poses to each item of data. And here's a quick way to re-use the work on the C.R.U.D. matrix we've already done. The numbers in the matrix – 1, 3, 9 – correspond to the entries in the C.R.U.D. matrix of Figure 1-6. Remember, the C.R.U.D. matrix was a mapping of use cases (rows) to data entities (columns), and what operation(s) each use case performed on the data in terms of data creation, reading, updating and deleting. For the QFD matrix of Figure 2-11, to get a quick and dirty estimate of severity, we simple reuse the body of the C.R.U.D. matrix of Figure 1-6, and replace all Cs and Ds with a 9 (bugs related to data creation and deletion would probably be severe); all Us we replace with 3 (bugs related to data updates would probably be moderately severe); and all Rs with 1 (bugs related to simply reading data would probably be of minor severity).

This is of course just one example of how to relatively rank severity; you might well decide to use an alternate scale ( perhaps you can put a dollar figure to severity in your application ), and it may well be the case that bugs related to reading data might be quite severe. This will all depend on your application.

The bottom row of the QFD matrix of Figure 2-11 then computes the risk exposure of each data entity based on both the relative frequency and relative severity. In our example, data entities Check Out Requests and Reservation Requests have high relative risk exposures. In Chapter 3 we'll utilize this information (what are the high risk data entities) in terms of the data lifecycle testing we design tests for. Then later in Chapter 9, *Example: Return Books Use Case, Reservation Requests Queue,* we'll brainstorm additional tests for Reservation Requests by virtue of modeling the reservation queue.

Figure 2-11 A QFD matrix provides a quick way to estimate risk exposure of data entities

| Use Cases | Relative Frequency | Data Entities | | | | | | | | |
|---|---|---|---|---|---|---|---|---|---|---|
| | | Titles | Copies of Books | Check Out Requests | Reservation Requests | Branch Library Transfers | Borrowers | Librarians | Curators | Branch Libraries |
| Add Books to Library Database | 0.011% | 9 | 9 | | 3 | | | | 1 | |
| Remove Books from Library Database | 0.001% | 1 | 9 | 9 | 1 | 9 | | | | |
| Do Book Search | 44% | 1 | 1 | 1 | 1 | 1 | 1 | 1 | 1 | |
| Lend Books | 23% | 1 | 1 | 9 | 3 | 1 | 1 | 1 | | |
| Return Books | 23% | 1 | 1 | 3 | 3 | | 1 | 1 | | |
| Reserve Books | 4% | 1 | 1 | 1 | 9 | | 1 | 1 | 1 | |
| Cancel Book Reservations | 4% | 1 | 1 | | 3 | | 1 | 1 | 1 | |
| Manage Book Transfers | 0.4% | 1 | 1 | 1 | 1 | 9 | | | 1 | 1 |
| Risk Exposure of Data Entities | | 0.99 | 0.99 | 3.24 | 2.30 | 0.71 | 0.98 | 0.98 | 0.52 | 0.004 |

=SUMPRODUCT($C$4:$C$11,F4:F11)

## LOAD & STRESS TESTING

We conclude this chapter with one additional use of the operational profile, design of load and stress tests.

Load and stress testing are tests performed on a system to determine its performance under expected work-loads and beyond (the stress part). This type of testing frequently involves the use of a tool such as HP's LoadRunner, or IBM Rational's Performance Tester that allow the tester to simulate use of the system by lots of users.

These tools work by allowing the tester to record use case scenarios, like those from the library management system example, then re-play them concurrently for hours or even days using tens to hundreds (or more!) "virtual users".

A key bit of test design for load and stress testing is identifying the user workloads, and an operational profile is just the ticket for this. Let's look at a couple examples for our library management system.

## Load Testing

Load testing seeks to demonstrate that a system can handle expected loads -- e.g. the expected number of concurrent users -- in a performant fashion, say measured in user response times.

Let's say for our library management system we want to schedule a one hour load test. Because we know the load is going to vary over a 24 hour period, we decide to test for the heaviest one hour load of the day and decide that our system needs to be able to handle as much as 20% of the daily load in a one hour period. Figure 2-12 illustrates how we might use the operational profile to estimate the loads we'll need to simulate. Using a product like HP Load Runner, we'd then calibrate each use case script to run the specified number of transaction (column 2) in that one hour period, while also monitoring system response times.

| Use Case | Times per day Executed | Load test: 20% of daily load in one hour |
|---|---|---|
| Do Book Search | 2110 | 422 |
| Lend Books | 1100 | 220 |
| Return Books | 1100 | 220 |
| Reserve Books | 211 | 43 |
| Cancel Book Reservations | 211 | 43 |
| Manage Book Transfers | 20 | 4 |
| Add Books to Library Database | 0.5 | 1 |
| Remove Books from Library Database | 0.05 | 1 |

Figure 2-12 Load test for ability to handle 20% of days load in one hour

## Stress Test

Whereas a load test usually tests a system at some expected load, it doesn't provide a look at the dynamics of system performance beyond that point, to see for example how much additional capacity the system has, say for growth. For this you need what I call a "ramping stress test".

The system is tested with a load that is ramped gradually from low to high, all the while monitoring performance to spot key points in the performance curve: the range where increasing load increases overall throughput without impacting user response times (the system has capacity to spare); the range where increasing load continues to increases overall throughput, but now at the expense of user response times; and ultimately the point beyond which throughput tops out and response times for users begin to climb (the system is maxed out).

Figure 2-13 illustrates the use of the operational profile for setting up such a ramping stress test in IBM's Rational Performance Tester. We setup a one hour test that ramps the load from 25 simulated users, to 50, to 75, and finally to 100. At each stage, the load is held steady for 15 minutes to allow a good performance baseline to be captured (see tab User Load; this is graphically illustrated in window User Load Preview).

Additionally, at each stage, the number of simulated users is allocated to each use case according to the relative frequency from our operational profile (see left window)[22].

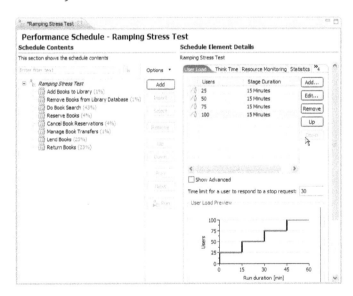

Figure 2-13 Using relative frequency from operational profile in running a ramping stress test

---

[22] Rational Performance Tester does not allow for fractions of a percent so I've rounded operational profile fractions up to 1%, and dropped the percentage for Do Book Search by a percent so that all sum to 100%, but you get the idea!

## CHAPTER REVIEW

In the previous chapter we looked at a tool – the C.R.U.D. matrix – to help evaluate the test adequacy of use case diagrams ("Are we missing any use cases we need for testing?"). Still working at the use case diagram level, in this chapter we looked at another tool – the operational profile – as a way to help you, the tester, concentrate on the most frequently used use cases, and hence those having a greater chance of failure in the hands of the user.

To generate the operational profile we looked at how to translate the use case diagram into a QFD matrix, allowing us to quantify the execution of each use case by the actors.

The chapter concluded with ways to use the operational profile, providing examples in terms of budgeting your time in test design (timeboxing), analyzing the risk exposure of use cases and data, and in load and stress testing.

# Chapter 3 Testing Use Cases of a Use Case Diagram in Concert

In Chapter 1 we looked at how to use a C.R.U.D. matrix to determine if there were any use cases we might want to add to the use case diagram to improve test adequacy. We noted that the process of working through the C.R.U.D. matrix was an important as the matrix itself, providing "Ah, Ha!" moments with valuable insight into the testing of the product. When completed the C.R.U.D. matrix was essentially a high level test case for the entire system, providing expected inputs (read), and outputs (create, update, delete) for the entire system in a compact, succinct form.

In Chapter 2 we then utilized the use case diagram to develop an operational profile to help with a bit of test planning, identifying high trafficked use cases in the system, high risk data, and even design of load and stress tests.

Still working at the use case diagram level – the 30,000-foot view of the system – a good next step in test design is to ask how the use cases of the diagram should be tested in concert.

This chapter will review testing techniques that you can apply to the use case diagram for this, i.e. integration testing of the use cases.

## Integration Testing Use Cases: from The Actors' Perspective

One obvious way to approach integration testing of use cases is from the perspective of one or more of the actors in the use case diagram. If pressed for time in test design, one might select the view point of a subset of the actors that collectively cover all the use cases in the diagram.

For example, referring to the use case diagram of Figure 1-7, one might choose to integration test all use cases from the viewpoints of the Self Service Kiosk and Book Curator actors. In doing so all use cases would be exercised.

Looking ahead in the book, In Chapter 4 we'll be learning about a technique called a Control Flow Graph. It's a great tool for designing tests based on sequences of "things". As it applies here the sequence we'd like to analyze and design tests for is the of sequence of use cases that an actor would be expected to execute.

As control flow graphs are thoroughly covered in Chapter 4, at this point suffice it to say that the same test design techniques that work for analyzing and designing tests for various sequences of use case steps works just the same for the sequencing of use cases themselves.

## INTEGRATION TESTING USE CASES: THE DATA'S PERSPECTIVE

An alternate strategy for the integration testing of use cases – the one we'll focus on in this chapter -- is from the perspective of the underlying data. This approach has the advantage that it can yield tests that cross actor boundaries; so not only testing use cases in concert, *but actors as well*.

And best of all, the effort expended on analysis to develop a C.R.U.D. matrix like that in Figure 1-6 can be re-used to develop tests for integration testing the use cases.

### DATA LIFECYCLE TESTING

Martin Pol et.al.'s[23] book provides a good description of how to design tests from a C.R.U.D. matrix, which they call "data cycle testing". Tests are designed to exercise data across its lifecycle, from initial creation, to subsequent use -- reading and updating -- to eventually being deleted.

Using the C.R.U.D. matrix from Figure 1-6 as an example, one begins by selecting a data entity (columns of the C.R.U.D. matrix) from which tests are to be designed. Ideally one would design tests for each data entity (what Martin Pol et.al. prescribes). In a pinch for time, however, one might focus on data entities most critical to the system.

In Chapter 2's section Risk Exposure and Data, we identified two "high risk" data entities, Check Out Requests and Reservation Requests. Let's look at data lifecycle

---

[23] Pol et.al., *Software Testing*

testing for these two, starting with Check Out Requests (we'll also visit Reservation Requests in Chapter 9, *Example: Return Books Use Case, Reservation Requests Queue* to illustrate brainstorming tests for queues).

## CHECK OUT REQUESTS EXAMPLE

Figure 3-1 shows the use cases from the C.R.U.D. matrix of Figure 1-6 that create, read, update or delete data entity Check Out Requests.

|  | Check Out Requests |
|---|---|
| Remove Books from Library Database | R, D |
| Do Book Search | R |
| Lend Books | R, C |
| Return Books | R, U |
| Reserve Books | R |
| Manage Book Transfers | R |

Figure 3-1 Use Cases that exercise Check Out Requests

To design data lifecycle tests for Check Out Requests, we can use a simple process based on three basic steps:

1. Create data (in this case a Check Out Request), then read to verify correctness
2. Update data (i.e. a Check Out Request), then read to verify changes
3. Delete data (i.e. a Check Out Request), then try to read to verify the data is really gone

Applying this three step process to the use cases of Figure 3-1 the following combination of use cases could, for example, be used to data lifecycle test Check Out Requests:

1) (Create) Lend a copy or copies of a book, then

a) Do a search on that book; Confirm checked out status
b) Reserve a copy for pickup at the library; You shouldn't get a copy checked out
c) Try to transfer a checked out book to another library; You should be prevented from this

2) (Update) Return a book that was checked out
a) Do a search and confirm the book status is now checked in
b) Reserve a book for which all copies were formerly checked out; you should be able to get the copy that was just checked in
c) Transfer to another library a copy of a book that formerly checked out, but has just been checked back in.

3) (Delete) Delete all copies of a book from the library (remember, the title remains); doing this removes all check out records for those copies.
a) Do a search and confirm no copies are available
b) Confirm you can't reserve these deleted books
c) Confirm you can't transfer these deleted copies to another library

## UPPING THE RIGOR WITH A STATE TRANSITION DIAGRAM

This approach to testing use cases in concert is based essentially on state transition testing which *"allows the tester to view the .. software in terms of its states, transition between states, and the inputs and events that trigger state changes"*[24]

As it applies to testing use cases in concert based on a data entity, the different configurations (values) of a data entity are what constitute "state". Creating, updating or deleting the data entity result in the "transitions between states". The use cases are the description of the "inputs and events" that trigger the transitions, and also the means of verifying expected results (state changes and outputs).

For data entity Check Out Requests the number of states, and the transitions between them are relatively straightforward: any particular check out request record goes from being non-existent, to checked out, to checked back in (and retained for historical book keeping for some period of time), to eventually being deleted, i.e. back to being non-existent.

---

[24] Ilene Burnstein, *Practical Software Testing: A Process-Oriented Approach,* 2010

Sometimes the state transitions are not so trivial and a state transition diagram can be used by the tester to map out the data entity's life-cycle, and the role each use case plays in moving from one state to the next. In the literature[25], this state transition diagram is variously called the *entity lifecycle diagram* or *entity life history diagram*. It's a perfect companion to the C.R.U.D. matrix, mirroring the create, read, update and delete theme in state transition diagram form.

A side note is in order here. The diagram that is produced is sometimes done as a *tree diagram*. Michael Jackson[26] notes *"..both notations are capable of describing exactly the same strings .. you can derive a tree diagram from any finite-state machine, and vice versa ..",* both having advantages over the other.

The state transition diagram is more common in testing literature, and in particular from the standpoint of this book, the state transition diagram is preferable in that I'm using the same notation – that of a directed graph – for state transition diagrams (this chapter), control flow graphs (Chapter 4), and syntax diagrams (Chapter 7). As such, the state transition diagram will have all the advantages discussed in Chapter 4's section Control Flow Graphs: Adjusting the Rigor of Test Design.

## Reservation Requests Example

Figure 3-2 shows the use cases from the C.R.U.D. matrix of Figure 1-6 that create, read and update data entity Reservation Requests. For constructing a state transition diagram, we can keep things simple by focusing on just those use cases that create, update or delete data (highlighted in Figure 3-2).

You can add in the use cases that simply read the data entity (un-highlighted in Figure 3-2), but they tend to clutter up the diagram with state transitions that don't "go anywhere", i.e. they immediately loop back to the state they start from (simply reading the data entity does not change the data entity, hence is not a transition to a

---

[25] One of the earliest papers using this technique is C. J. Rosenquist, *Entity Life Cycle Models and Their Applicability to Information Systems Development Life Cycles.* Comput. J. 25(3): 307-315 (1982)

[26] Michael Jackson, *Software Requirements & Specification: A Lexicon of Practice, Principles and Prejudices*, Addison-Wesley, 1995

new state). My preference is to keep the diagram simple, and just keep in mind that that these use cases that simply read the data entity need to be tested on appropriate states.

Returning to Figure 1-6, remember that while book reservations are created and updated, no use cases delete the backlog of old reservations. This was identified as a missing use case, but one we marked as "don't care". So for Reservation Requests we need only focus on use cases that create or update a reservation request; these are highlighted in Figure 3-2.

| | Reservation Requests |
|---|---|
| Add Books to Library Database | U |
| Remove Books from Library Database | R |
| Do Book Search | R |
| Lend Books | R, U |
| Return Books | R, U |
| Reserve Books | C |
| Cancel Book Reservations | U |
| Manage Book Transfers | R |
| DON'T CARE | D |

Figure 3-2 Use Cases that exercise data entity Reservation Requests

The idea is to build a state transition diagram; A directed graph that shows how the identified use cases of Figure 3-2 take a reservation request from one state to another, from start to end. State transition diagrams have a reputation for getting really big and unmanageable (state space explosion). But as used here – to model the lifecycle of a single data entity – the diagrams will typically be small.

Figure 3-3 shows such a state transition diagram for data entity Reservation Request. The various states of a reservation are shown as nodes (circles) in the graph. Lines with arrows, called edges of the graph, show the transitions from one state to the next; these we label with the highlighted use cases from Figure 3-2 (those which *affect* state changes, i.e. those that create, update or delete data).

Our state transition diagram for the reservation request (indeed any data entity) will always have *one start* and *one end state* that denote a reservation request *before* creation, and *after* eventual deletion, respectively.

Notice that neither edge leading to the end state has been labeled with a use case. This was a hole in our uses cases we previously identified, i.e. while book reservations are created, read and updated by the use cases, none delete the backlog of old reservations (refer back to Figure 1-6). This does point out that building a state transition diagram is another useful tool for spotting missing use cases, i.e. are there states with edges leading to them for which we have no use case to label them?

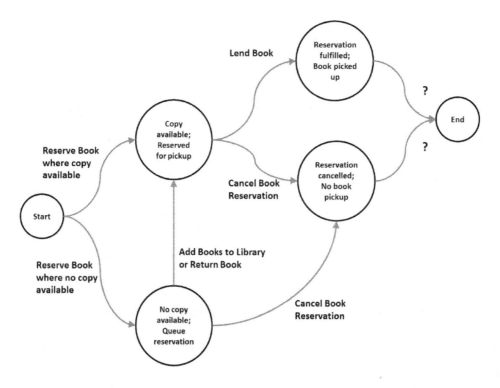

Figure 3-3 State Transition Diagram for data entity Reservation Request. Question marks indicate known missing use cases for these state transitions.

With state transition diagram in place, tests are designed to integrate (execute use cases in concert) in two ways:

1. Use cases appearing as labels on the edges (the highlighted use cases of Figure 3-2) are executed in sequence to cover the states and transitions of the graph.
2. At each state one or more use cases are executed that would read and verify the correctness of the data entity at that state (the un-highlighted use cases of Figure 3-2).

With regards to item #1, because a state transition diagram is a directed graph, all the test design techniques we'll cover in Chapter 4 on control flow graphs will apply here. This includes the ability to make estimates on the number of tests we'll need[27], and to adjust the rigor of test design as appropriate, testing lots of paths through state transition diagrams of data entities identified as "high risk" (see Chapter 2), and not so many paths through diagrams for data at less risk.

## CHAPTER REVIEW

Here's a review of what we discussed in this chapter.

In Chapter 1 we looked at how to use a C.R.U.D. matrix to determine if there were any use cases we might want to add to the use case diagram to improve test adequacy. In Chapter 2 we then utilized the improved use case diagram to develop an operational profile to spot high trafficked use cases in the system. Still working at the use case diagram level this chapter covered a good next step in test design: How to test the use cases of the use case diagram in concert, i.e. use case integration testing.

We began with a brief discussion of testing use cases in concert from the perspective of actors. But the focus of this chapter was the integration testing of use cases from the perspective of underlying data. This approach has the advantage that it can yield tests that cross actor boundaries; so not only testing use cases in concert, *but actors as well*.

Using the C.R.U.D. matrix from Figure 1-6, we saw how to do what Martin Pol et.al. call data lifecycle testing and concluded the chapter with looking at how to up the rigor of data lifecycle testing by use of a state transition diagram.

---

[27] Having exactly *one start and one end* is key to estimating the number of needed tests. For Figure 3-3 we can estimate the need four tests, give or take based on the rigor desired. We'll cover this in Chapter 4.

# PART II: THE USE CASE

## TEST DESIGN FROM 20,000 FEET

Uses cases provide a way to decompose test design into levels of test, not based on units, but rather paths through the system. In Part I of the book we approached test design from what I've called the 30,000-foot level of test. At that level, paths through the system are in terms of traffic trod across a whole set of use cases, those belonging to the use case diagram.

In this, Part II, we'll drop down to 20,000 feet and look at black-box techniques to apply to those high priority use cases we identified at the 30,000-foot level ( You may want to refer back to the strategy laid out back in Figure 0-4).

 At this, the 20,000-foot level of test, paths through the system are in terms of paths through an individual use case.

Chapter 4 discusses Control Flow Graphs (CFG), a model based on graph theory of the paths through "something". In testing their earliest use was for designing tests to cover the various paths through a program's code; this is white-box testing. But they are equally useful in black-box test design and are an effective tool for designing tests based on paths through a use case.

For use case based testing, control flow graphs have a lot going for them, easy to learn, work nicely with risk driven testing (high frequency paths correlate with high risk). There are, however, other test techniques that work well at this level of use case testing ( identifying the paths through a use case to be tested). Chapter 5 looks at two alternate techniques for working with use cases at this level of test: decision tables, and pairwise testing.

# Chapter 4 CONTROL FLOW GRAPHS

Control Flow Graphs (CFG) are a model, based on graph theory, of the paths through "something". In testing their earliest use was as a basis for designing tests to cover the various paths through a program's code; this is white-box testing.

But they are also useful in black-box test design, writing tests based on the specified behavior of a component [28].  And as it relates to the task at hand, CFGs have proven an effective tool for test design when the specified behavior is via use cases [29].

 Leffingwell and Widrig[30] in their chapter "From Use Cases to Test Cases" frame  well the problem we'll address in this chapter:

*"As we move [from use cases] into test cases .. we need to think in terms of specific scenarios that occur for each use case .. [Each path through a use case] .. is a scenario, or use case instance,  that can be both executed and tested .. In understanding this, we also come to understand one of the most significant challenges with system testing: even with a limited number of use cases, a large number of specific scenarios must be tested .."*

Control flow graphs provide a way to address this problem, allowing the tester to scale the rigor of test design up or down in relation to the criticality of the use case.

## DEVELOPING THE CONTROL FLOW GRAPH

The great thing about CFGs is that their visual orientation makes them intuitive to learn and use. Let's jump in with an example from the library book management system introduced in Part I.

---

[28] Boris Beizer, *Software Testing Techniques*, 2nd edition, 1990
[29] Armour and Miller, *Advanced Use Case Modeling*
[30] Dean Leffingwell & Don Widrig, *Managing Software Requirements*, 2nd edition, *A Use Case Approach*, 2003

In Chapter 2 we developed an operational profile of the library management system and discovered that 90% of the use case activity is accounted for by just three use cases: **Do Book Search**, **Lend Books**, and **Return Books**.

Using the strategy we outlined in the preface to this book -- start at the "top" and work our way down, spending time at each level designing tests for the critical bits at that level -- the use case **Do Book Search** looks to be a good next step in test design so let's build a CFG for that use case.

Figure 4-1 presents the textual description of the **Do Book Search** use case, including a basic flow and alternate flows. It is these we want to model as a control flow graph.

## Use Case: **Do Book Search**

Allows authenticated librarians, book curators and borrowers to search for books.

## Basic Flow

- User logs in on the library's home page using ID and password.
- User clicks on link titled "Search Library Catalog". System navigates to the catalog search page.
- User species how they want to search, by author or title.
- User types keywords into the search field, then hits submit.
- System responds with a list of titles that match the query.
- User logs out.

## Alternate Flows

- At login, if authentication fails, clear ID and password and let user try again. Alternatively, the user can click on the "Get Help With Login" link that will navigate to the customer service page (ending this use case).
- Each user account has a profile that includes different permission sets based on whether the user is a curator, librarian (could be both), or "just" a library patron. After login, if the user is a curator, display the curator "message of the day", a common message sent curators keeping them abreast of late

breaking information. If the user is (also) a librarian, display the librarian message of the day as well.

- On the catalog search page, the user can repeat the search process as many times as desired.
- If a search fails to find any results, the system responds with a "No results found" message, and provides helpful tips on searching. The user is then allowed to search again.

Figure 4-1 Basic and alternate flows for use case Do Book Search

Figure 4-2 shows a CFG for the **Do Book Search** use case of Figure 4-1. Using this example, let's walk through the main bits that make up a CFG. [31]

First, the CFG needs to have one start, and one end (shown as circles). More on this in a moment.

The squares in our graph are called "nodes" which represent a block of one or more consecutive (non-branching) use case steps. It's worth emphasizing, you don't need to have one node for each and every step of the use case. One node can represent a block of steps where the flow of control is straight through. The whole reason behind a control flow graph is to model paths through the use case; if steps follow one after another they are on the same path and one node is sufficient to model them in the graph.

Lines with arrows are called "arcs", or directed "edges" of the graph, and show the possible sequential flow of control through blocks of use case steps (nodes). Because the edges have direction, a control flow graph is what is called a *directed graph*. Nodes with multiple exiting edges denote decision points where the flow will take one branch or another.

In a CFG, the interior areas bounded by the edges are called "regions"; in our graph of Figure 4-2 the regions have been numbered 1 through 7. Getting a count of the regions is why we make sure the CFG has exactly one start and one end. Notice that

---

[31] If you need additional help on deriving a control flow graph from a use case, see Armour and Miller, *Advanced Use Case Modeling* for some simple tips.

in our example here, the use case had two exit points, which then connect to a common end. In doing so we created region 6. Knowing the number of regions in the graph is important for the tester, and we'll be discussing this more later.

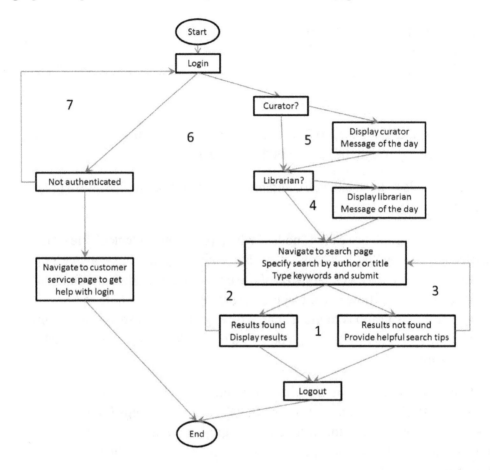

Figure 4-2 Control flow graph for Do Book Search use case

CONTROL FLOW GRAPHS: ADJUSTING THE RIGOR OF TEST DESIGN

Besides being intuitive to develop, describing how to use them in test design is straightforward. As Beizer is famously quoted, *"What do you [as a tester] do when you see a graph? Cover it!"*[32]

But remember that in this chapter on control flow graphs, we are addressing what Leffingwell and Widrig called a significant challenge with system testing, i.e. *"..even with a limited number of use cases, a large number of specific scenarios[ paths thru the use case ] must be tested .."*

So in "covering it" (the control graph of the use case) it is in deciding *how* to cover it the tester has the ability to adjust rigor to need, testing lots of paths through frequently used use cases, and not so many paths through others.

In this section we are going to illustrate how to "turn up or down" the test design "rigor knob" using the CFG of **Do Book Search** (Figure 4-2). Just keep in mind we already know that from our operational profile in Figure 2-2 this use case is frequently used, so would normally need more rigor than less. Never the less, using a single CFG is the best way to illustrate adjusting rigor (coverage) to need.

Let's begin with the least rigorous coverage, and step it up from there.

Before diving in however let's re-draw our graph of Figure 4-2, replacing the descriptive text in nodes with numbers to facilitate discussing paths through the graph. For the balance of the examples in this section we'll be referring to the graph of Figure 4-3 .

---

[32] Boris Beizer, *Black-Box Testing, Techniques for Functional Testing of Software and Systems,* 1995

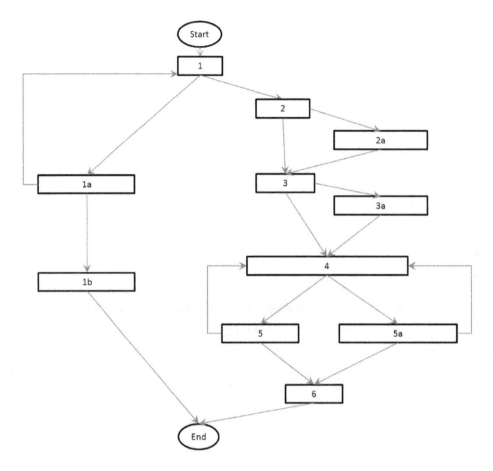

Figure 4-3 The use case control flow graph of Figure 4-2 with text in nodes replaced by numbers to facilitate discussion of paths through the graph.

## "HAPPY PATH" COVERAGE

If from our operational profile we determine that our use case is rarely used (or otherwise have decided is not critical) the least coverage we'd want to afford it is a test or tests to exercise the basic flow, sometimes called the "happy path" through the use case. Tests, plural? Right, one path may have multiple tests, e.g. with varying inputs using techniques we'll be covering in Part III of the book.

The use case basic flow for the **Do Book Search** use case (described in Figure 4-1) is described as this path through the graph of Figure 4-3 :

- 1, 2, 3, 4, 5, 6

This happy path through the control flow graph is easily mapped to the action / expected-result test format of tools like Quality Center shown in Figure 0-1.

The key point in terms of control flow is that the test case is designed to take the desired path through the decision points of the graph. For example, in order to cover the happy path the test must be designed to use an ID to by-pass the display of curator and librarian messages of the day, and the search must be designed to look for a book that is known to exist in the library. A sample test case that illustrates this is shown in Figure 4-4.[33]

| Step | Description | Expected Result |
|---|---|---|
| Login | User logins in on library homepage with a valid user ID and password that is set up as a regular librarian patron with *no* curator or librarian permissions. | System successfully authenticates user, displaying "Hello .." greeting.<br><br>System recognizes user is not a curator or librarian, and hence no curator / librarian message of the day is displayed. |
| Navigate to search page. | User clicks on link titled "Search Library Catalog". | System displays the search page. |
| Search | User types keywords from the title of a book of interest. | System finds all books with titles that contain the keywords, and displays them in list form. |
| Logout | User clicks on logout link at top of page. | System logs out the user, displaying the "Goodbye .." message. |

Figure 4-4 Test case for "happy path" of Do Book Search use case

---

[33] We'll be beefing up this test with input testing later in the book; see Example 2: Syntax Testing for Do Book Search Use Case.

## NODE COVERAGE

Happy path coverage would be the least rigorous coverage a test or tests would afford a control flow graph. Next let's turn up the rigor knob just a bit.

Recall that nodes of our graph represent a block of one or more consecutive (non-branching) use case steps. Our next step up in coverage rigor would be to identify a path or paths that cover all those nodes, i.e. node coverage. For each of those paths, you'd then write one or more tests for each, just as we did for "happy path" coverage.

We can achieve node coverage of the graph of Figure 4-3 with tests to cover as few as 2 paths

- 1, 2, 2a, 3, 3a, 4, 5, 4, 5a, 6
- 1, 1a, 1b

## EDGE COVERAGE

To summarize thus far, "happy path" coverage of a use case's control flow graph is achieved by writing a test or tests for the basic flow through the use case (one path). Node coverage ups the ante on test coverage by requiring enough tests to ensure every node of the graph is covered; for our **Do Book Search** control flow graph we can do this with tests for as few as two paths.

Notice that even with full node coverage, however, there were certain edges of the graph that remained uncovered, namely

- edge 2, 3
- edge 3, 4
- edge 1a, 1
- edge 5a, 4
- edge 5, 6

If we keep in mind that an "edge" represents flow of control through the use case, we see the significance of this: Nodes with multiple exiting edges denote decision points where the flow will take one branch or another. An edge that remains uncovered represents a decision outcome that has not been tested.

80

So if we have a use case that warrants even more rigor, our next step up would be edge coverage. For our graph of Figure 4-3 we can achieve edge coverage by testing as few as three paths:

- 1, 2, 2a, 3, 3a, 4, 5, 4, 5a, 4, 5, 6
- 1, 2, 3, 4, 5a, 6
- 1, 1a, 1, 1a, 1b

Notice in our example that as we've up the requirements of coverage – happy path, node, edge – the number of paths we need to test has increased from 1 to 2 to 3, respectively.

By judiciously choosing which use cases will get which level of coverage, the test designer controls the number of tests that get written, writing more where the bang for the buck is greatest, and writing fewer where it is less.

## BASIS PATH COVERAGE

Where full node coverage still left certain edges of the graph uncovered, it's possible (likely) that full edge coverage will not cover all paths through the graph.

As we have just seen, while we can achieve edge coverage by testing as few as three paths, the graph of Figure 4-3 has thirty-four (34) paths (and an infinite number if we are willing to endlessly loop through cycles such as 4,5,4 and 4,5a,4 to derive new paths).

Where as the number of paths to be tested did not increase unreasonably from a testing standpoint as we moved from "happy path" coverage, to node coverage, to edge coverage, when we step up to covering all the paths of a graph, the number of paths will often be so high as to be infeasible for testing.

So if testing all paths is often not feasible, what is?

A good compromise to all paths testing is basis path testing or basis path coverage, i.e. test a set of basis paths, also known as a basis set. A basis set is a minimal set of " independent paths" such that all other paths can be expressed in terms of this minimal set. A basis set is minimal in the sense that were you to remove any one of the paths from a basis set, you would not be able to express all the paths of the flow graph with the remaining paths. [34]

From a testing perspective the basis set is important in the sense that, as Jorgensen[35] puts it *"If the basis is OK, we could hope that everything that can be expressed in terms of the basis is also OK"*.

Another important aspect of basis path coverage: Like edge coverage, it will ensure that every decision outcome is covered (and hence every node also). But unlike edge coverage, it ups the rigor of testing by making sure that each decision is tested *independently*.

The importance of this for testing is best illustrated with a very simple example.[36] Let's say we have some use case with a control flow graph that looks something like the one in Figure 4-5. Again we'll use numbered nodes as an easy way to talk about paths. We can achieve edge coverage of this graph by testing as few as two paths:

- 1, 2, 3 (presumably our "happy path")
- 1, 1a, 2, 2a, 3

But now let's say we know a bit more about this use case; that there's some quantity X (widgets, dollars or whatever) that should *not* be changed by this use case. Let's then suppose that at the code level, a couple of faults creep into the implementation of our use case, namely the code associated with step 1a increments X by 1, and that of step 2a decrements X by 1; this too is illustrated in Figure 4-5.

---

[34] A basis set need not be unique for a flow graph; there can be multiple basis sets. The details of how one proves that all paths are expressible by a basis set involves a deep dive into linear algebra (matrix theory) which may, or may not, find useful from a work-a-day testing perspective. If you are interested in tackling this, see Paul Jorgensen, *Software Testing: A Craftsman's Approach,* 3rd edition, 2008

[35] Jorgensen, *Software Testing: A Craftsman's Approach*

[36] Based on example from Arthur H. Watson and Thomas J. McCabe, *Structured Testing: A Testing Methodology Using the Cyclomatic Complexity Metric*, NIST Special Publication 500-235, 1996

It should be clear from Figure 4-5 that testing the two paths we have chosen for edge cover will not catch the fact that the code is manipulating X. The first path circumvents the faulty code, and the second is such that separate faults mask one another.

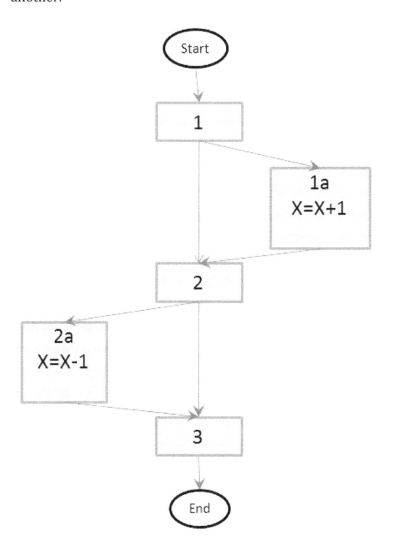

Figure 4-5 Separate faults in the code implementing steps 1a and 2a can interact such that one masks detection of the other

While this example is contrived to make this problem very obvious, the problem is real enough.

A basis set of paths prevents this problem because the paths are such that each decision is tested *independently* from all others. What does that mean? I like to think of it like this: It's the same principle as in a controlled science experiment where you carefully change only one variable in the experiment at a time, keeping everything else constant. In that way, you test the outcome of that change independent of all other variables in the experiment.

In a basis set, each path has a matching path that is just like it, *except* for one and only one decision. For that one decision on which they differ, one path tests one outcome, and the second path tests another. All other aspects of their route are the same.

Deriving a basis set is straightforward ( easier than describing what they are! ). The following is based on McCabe's "baseline method" for coming up with a basis set. He used the term "baseline" to describe some initial path selected by the tester which represents the "baseline functionality" being tested. Today's testers would know this as the use case basic flow, or "happy path", so this method works great for control flow graphs of use cases.

### Basis Path Coverage for the Do Book Search Control Flow Graph

Let's return to the control graph of the **Do Book Search** use case shown in Figure 4-2 and derive a basis set for this graph using roughly the same technique described in McCabe's baseline method. I find it easiest to describe this process with a series of snapshots of the graph as path by path is derived for a basis set.

Begin by identifying the path that corresponds to the use case's "happy path"; this is shown in Figure 4-6.

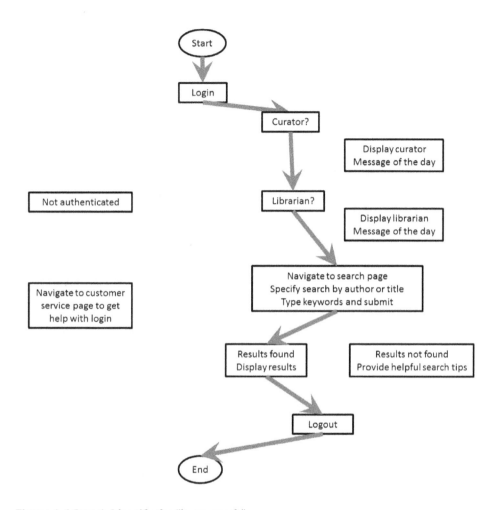

Figure 4-6 Step 1, Identify the "happy path"

Next we select one – and only one – decision point and explore an alternate outcome. This is shown in Figure 4-7 where a dotted line shows the newly explored path. Notice it is identical to the previous path – in this case the HappyPath -- except for one decision outcome.

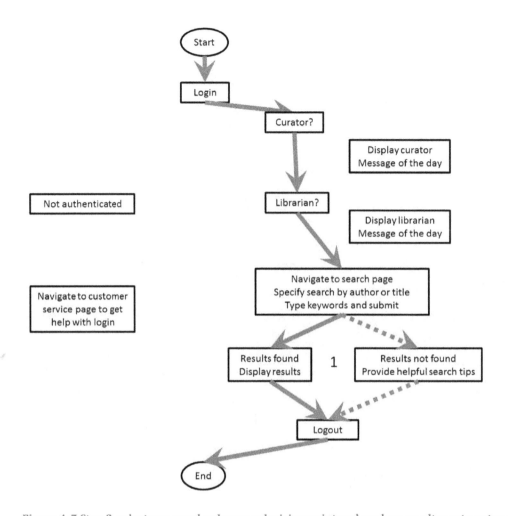

Figure 4-7 Step 2, select one – and only one – decision point and explore an alternate outcome

Notice that this new alternate path, combined with the first path ("happy path"), have now created an encircled region of the graph which has been numbered "1". You'll recall from earlier in this section that graphs are made of nodes, edges and regions. Regions are the areas bounded by edges of the graph.

Next we take one of the paths we have already created and again change one – and only one – decision outcome. This is Figure 4-8. This third path combined with the happy path has created an encircled region which has been numbered "2".

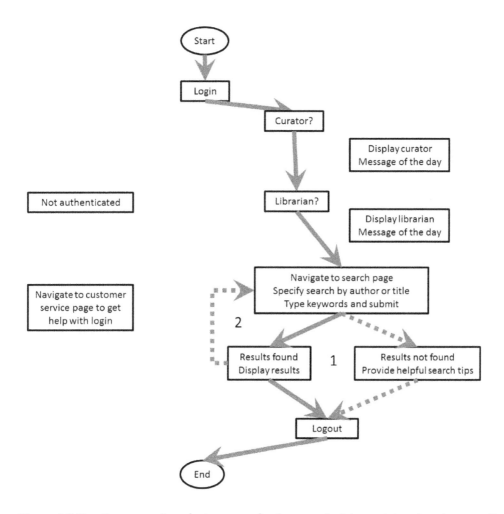

Figure 4-8 Step 3, once again, select one – and only one – decision point and explore an alternate outcome

This process is repeated – select a previous path, make one and only one change to a decision outcome – until we have added all the edges of the graph. Completed graph shown in Figure 4-9. Solid line shows the original happy path; Dotted lines the new paths that have been added.

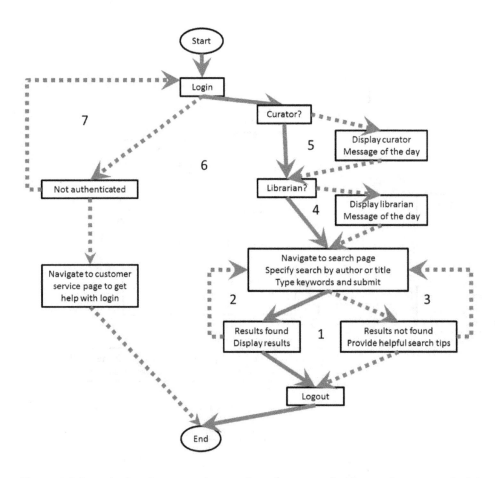

Figure 4-9, Iteratively select a previous path, make one and only one change to a decision outcome, until we have added all the edges of the graph. This is the final graph with all basis paths identified.

Snapshots of the complete eight step process are shown in Figure 4-10.

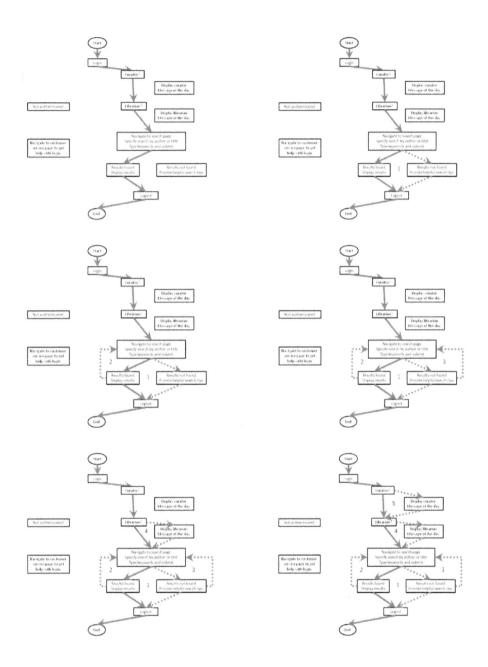

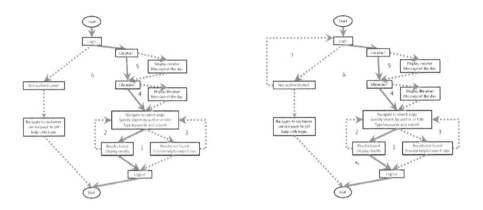

Figure 4-10 Snapshots showing all steps for deriving the basis set.

Notice that the number of paths in our basis set is 8, which turns out to be the number of regions plus 1. That's no accident and is one of the great things about basis path coverage.

Given a graph, if you count the regions and add 1, you can predict ahead of time how many paths any basis set for the graph will have. That number is called the "cyclomatic complexity" of the graph. Knowing the cyclomatic complexity gives the tester firm footing for test planning. The cyclomatic complexity is

- An *upper* bound number for the number of paths needed if you are shooting for edge coverage
- A *lower* bound number on the total number of paths
- *Equal* to the number of paths in any basis set which would be needed to test each decision independently.

## USE OF CONTROL FLOW GRAPH IN LOAD AND STRESS TESTING

In Chapter 2, From Use Case Diagram to Operational Profile, we looked at the use of an operational profile for planning load and stress testing, tests performed on a system to determine its performance under expected workloads and beyond (the stress part).

That chapter looked at deriving the operational profile for a set of use cases associated with a use case diagram. Sometimes, however, you need to perform a load or stress test based on the various scenarios of a single use case (Important note: Not planning on doing a load or stress test? This idea of developing an operational profile for a single use case is also useful for identifying the high priority paths to which the test design techniques of Part III of the book will be applied ).

This can be done by using the set of paths developed from the control flow graph for node, edge or basis path coverage, then quantifying the expected relative frequency of each path respective to one another. Let me illustrate with an example.

Figure 4-11 shows a control flow graph for a use case with numbered blocks representing blocks of steps in the use case; as before, this just makes it easier to talk about paths through the graph.

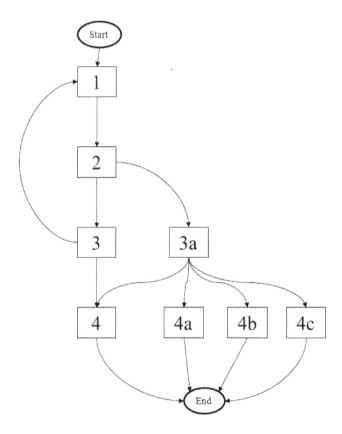

Figure 4-11 Sample control flow graph from which to generate an operational profile of paths through a use case

Using, say, the technique we discussed in the previous section, Basis Path Coverage, we can then identify these six paths that we want to use for load or stress testing ( and remember, we'll know ahead of time we need exactly 6 because the cyclomatic complexity of the graph is 5 + 1):

- 1, 2, 3, 4 ("happy path")
- 1, 2, 3, 1, 2, 3, 4
- 1, 2, 3a, 4
- 1, 2, 3a, 4a
- 1, 2, 3a, 4b
- 1, 2, 3a, 4c

Whereas previously we used the operational profile to show the relative amount of traffic between use cases of the use case diagram, now we'll construct an operational profile to show the relative traffic through these paths of a single use case.

We do this by turning our control flow graph into a *decision graph*. A decision graph is a means for calculating the probability of an event, in this case the probability that the user will take one path through the use case, over the next.

As Figure 4-12 illustrates, our use case of Figure 4-11 is easily converted to a decision graph model.

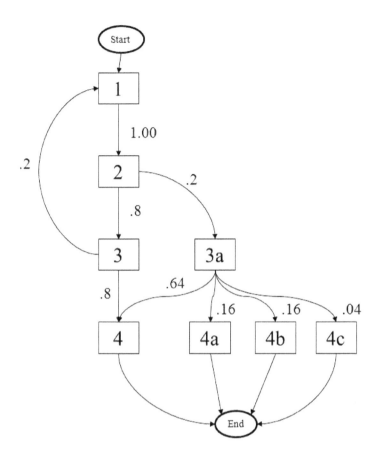

Figure 4-12 Converting the control flow graph to a decision graph of use case

In the decision graph of Figure 4-12 each edge leaving a node (block of steps in the use case) is assigned a probability. It is the probability with which we expect that edge to be used relative to alternate edges leaving the node. *The probability of all edges leaving a node must sum to 1.*

For example, after a user has executed the steps of node 2 in Figure 4-12 we expect that 80% of the time the user will go to node 3, and 20% of the time they will go to step 3a.

Once probabilities are assigned to each path, the probability of each scenario is calculated by taking the product of the probabilities of paths in that scenario. For example, the probability of path 1, 2, 3, 4 is :

$$1 \times .8 \times .8 = .64$$

What this means is that we expect this path (our "happy path") to receive 64% of user traffic through the use case. The probability of each path of Figure 4-12 is shown in Table 4-1.

| Scenario | Probability |
|---|---|
| 1, 2, 3, 4 | 0.64 |
| 1, 2, 3, 1 | 0.16 |
| 1, 2, 3a, 4 | 0.13 |
| 1, 2, 3a, 4a | 0.03 |
| 1, 2, 3a, 4b | 0.03 |
| 1, 2, 3a, 4c | 0.01 |
| TOTAL | 1.00 |

Table 4-1 Probability of each scenario of Figure 4-12

## QUICK, LOW-TECH APPROACH TO ASSIGNING PROBABILITIES

Without empirical results from the field or usability studies, the probabilities you use in your decision graph will likely be "guesstimates". Rather than spending a lot of time agonizing over the numbers, there's always the Pareto Principle that you might find useful to apply to the operational profile.

The term "Pareto Principle" (or Pareto Law or simply 80/20 rule) was coined by Joseph Juran in his *Quality Control Handbook*, first released in 1951. He based the term on the work of Italian economist Vilfredo Pareto who observed that in modeling the distribution of wealth and land, 80 percent was held by 20 percent of the population. Juran's original application of this distribution was applied to manufacturing where he observed that 80% of the problems reported stemmed from 20% of all types of defects. The Pareto Principle has subsequently proved a good model for many phenomena, both in the natural and social world, including software engineering with rules of thumb such as "20% of the modules contain 80% of the defects".

So when all else fails – you have no empirical data from the field, you don't have time for a usability study, and you are frustrated at guessing – you might find it useful to apply the Pareto Principle to operational profiles: 20% of the paths exiting a use case step will carry 80% of the user traffic.

## USING THE OPERATIONAL PROFILE LOAD AND STRESS TESTS

Back in Chapter *From Use Case Diagram to Operational Profile*, Figure 2-13 illustrated the use of an operational profile of a set of use cases for setting up a ramping stress test in IBM's Rational Performance Tester.

The same approach would be used here as well for a ramping stress test using the operational profile shown in Table 4-1 for the six paths of decision graph of Figure 4-12.

As illustrated here, we setup a one hour test that ramps the load from 25 simulated users, to 50, to 75, and finally to 100. At each stage, the load is held steady for 15 minutes to allow a good performance baseline to be captured. The probabilities from the operational profile are then used to specify what percentage of the load is to be allocated to the scripts that are simulating usage of each of the six paths of the use case.

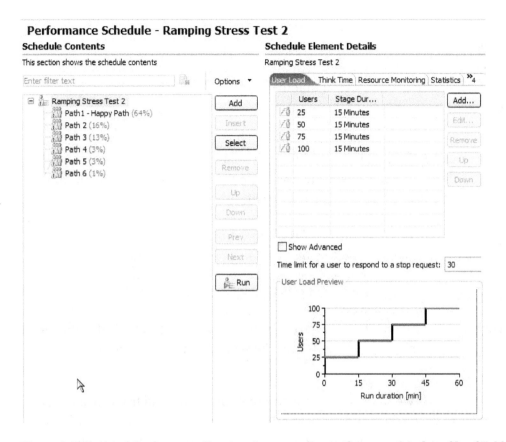

Figure 4-13 Rational Performance Tester setup according to the operational profile of Table 4-1

## Chapter Review

Let's review what we've talked about in this chapter.

The focus of Part II of this book is to drop down from test design and planning at the 30,000-foot level – that of the use case diagram – to the 20,000-foot level of test, where paths through the system are in terms of paths through an individual use case.

The tool discussed in this chapter for modeling paths through an individual use case was the Control Flow Graphs (CFG). The great thing about CFGs is that their visual orientation makes them intuitive to learn and use.

An additional advantage of CFGs is the ability to adjust rigor up or down based on how important a use case is. Four separate ways of "covering" the use case's CFG were discussed which increase rigor from low to high respectively: "happy path" coverage, node coverage, edge coverage, and basis path coverage.

The chapter concluded with a look at how to re-use the work done in developing a use case CFG for the purpose of load and stress testing the system.

# Chapter 5 ALTERNATE TECHNIQUES

For use case based testing, control flow graphs have a lot going for them:

- Generally easy to learn
- Dovetail nicely with risk driven testing (high frequency paths correlate with high risk)
- Can also be leveraged for load testing

There are, however, other test techniques that work well at this level of use case testing, i.e. for identifying the paths through a use case to be tested. In this brief chapter we'll look at two.

## DECISION TABLES

A decision table is *"a table showing combinations of inputs and/or stimuli (causes) with their associated outputs and/or actions (effects), which can be used to design Test Cases"*[37]

Notable applications of decision tables to use cases are Robert Binder's [38] Extended Use Case Test Design Pattern, and Leffingwell and Widrig's "test matrix" [39]

Here's an example of a decision table I bet you are familiar with! Figure 5-1 is part of a table for computing personal income tax in the United States.

---

[37] ISTQB Glossary
[38] Binder, *Testing Object-Oriented Systems*
[39] Leffingwell & Widrig, *Managing Software Requirements*

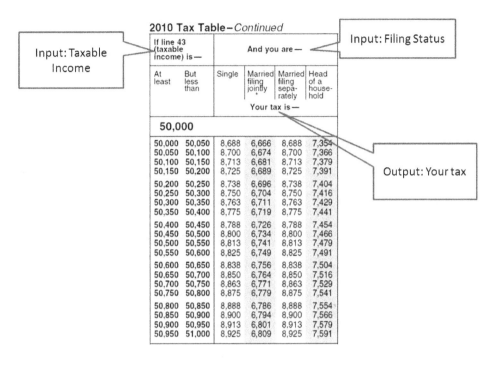

Figure 5-1 Table for computing personal income tax in the United States

The tax table of Figure 5-1 defines a relationship between two inputs – your *taxable income* and *filing status* (single, married filed jointly, married filing separately, and head of a house-hold) -- and the output (your tax).

Each row provides a different scenario in your own personal "paying taxes use case"; if your income meets the conditions predicated on the inputs (your income is "At least" X, "But less than" Y) that row outputs the tax rates that apply to you, for the various filing statuses. If you were testing a software program for doing personal income taxes, you might use a table such as this to specify the expected outputs of the program.

Table 5-1 is a decision table for describing the various scenarios of the **Do Book Search** use case of Figure 4-1. The first column of the table simply numbers each of the 6 use case scenarios.

The next 4 columns describe various states of the inputs to the use case: were the login ID and password valid? Is the user a curator? A Librarian? Were results found for book search query provided?

The last 2 columns describe the expected results for the various combinations of input states.

| Scenarios | Inputs | | | | Expected Result | |
|---|---|---|---|---|---|---|
| | Login ID and Password? | Curator? | Librarian? | Search Query? | Special Message(s) to User | Search Results |
| 1 | Valid | No | No | Found | None | Display all books that match search query |
| 2 | Valid | No | No | Not Found | Display message that no books match that query. Provide helpful search tips. | None |
| 3 | Valid | No | Yes | Found | Display librarian message of the day | Display all books that match search query |
| 4 | Valid | Yes | No | Found | Display curator message of the day | Display all books that match search query |

| Scenarios | Inputs | | | | Expected Result | |
|---|---|---|---|---|---|---|
| | Login ID and Password? | Curator? | Librarian? | Search Query? | Special Message(s) to User | Search Results |
| 5 | Valid | Yes | Yes | Found | Display both librarian and curator message of the day | Display all books that match search query |
| 6 | Failed | n/a | n/a | n/a | Login failed. Navigate to the customer service page to get help with login. | None |

Table 5-1 Decision table describing the various scenarios of Do Book Search use case

This decision table was developed from the control flow graph of Figure 4-2. This is similar to the test design approach described by Leffingwell and Widrig[40]. They begin with a control flow graph of the use case to identify the use case scenarios, then use the flow graph as a basis for developing what they call the "scenario matrix" from which their decision table evolves.

## DECISION TABLE DRAWBACKS?

Let's close the discussion on decision tables with some potential drawbacks to be aware of.

---

[40] Leffingwell & Widrig, *Managing Software Requirements*

One might argue that if you need to develop a control flow graph to aid in developing a decision table (process described by Leffingwell and Widrig ) why not simply apply the test design techniques that work directly on control flow graphs (previous chapter) skipping the development of a decision table?

An additional drawback to decision tables with respect to use cases is that the notion of looping is a bit hard to deal with in table format. Notice the decision table of Table 5-1 does not include scenarios in which looping takes place, e.g. scenario where user login first fails, user tries again and then succeeds.

Leffingwell and Widrig's address this with an additional "scenario matrix" that does manage to incorporate loops into a decision table format, but again it rests somewhat on having built a control flow graph of the use case to start with.

Another issue with decision tables as applied to use case scenarios: Decision tables are great for depicting the logic of a single bit of functionality. But a use case scenario, because of its workflow nature, may lump together several bits of functionality that aren't logically related ( it may be important to test them in concert via a use case scenario, but logically their behavior may be described independently). For example, in the **Do Book Search** decision table of Table 5-1, it's not immediately obvious from inspection of a single scenario – say scenario #3 – that the only factor that determines whether the system displays the librarian message of the day is whether the user is a properly logged in librarian.

To put it another way, if we view the rows of the table as records of a relational database, in database lingo the table is not properly "normalized". The table contains data items (columns) whose functional or multi-valued dependencies would normally be described by separate tables.

Compare this to the control flow graph of Figure 4-2; it's immediately obvious from inspection of the graph that display of the librarian message of the day is dependent solely on two factors: did the user get logged in, and is the user a librarian.

One final drawback to decision tables. Use cases are by their nature workflow oriented, often describing step-by-step procedures. This workflow information can be useful for testers during testing. This procedural knowledge is lost when the use case scenario is compressed to a row of a decision table.

Compare for example the test case for the "happy path" of the **Do Book Search** use case in Figure 4-4 (a direct reflection of the "happy path" through the control flow graph) with row #1 of the decision table of Table 5-1.

All these caveats aside, there are definitely times when the tester will reach for the decision table over (or combined with) the control flow graph; imagine trying to describe the tax table of Figure 5-1 solely as a control flow graph!

## PAIRWISE TESTING

In the previous section we saw how a decision table is used to describe the various paths through a use case to be tested. The decision table identifies as columns the various inputs to the use case; each row then shows the combination of input values that result in a particular path being taken.

The key point with a decision table is that there are dependencies between the inputs (columns) of the table, i.e. not all possible combinations of inputs describe a valid path through the use case. For some use cases, however, the various paths through a use case are determined by inputs that are independent of each other. Or put another way, any (or most) combination of input values is valid, and results in a path through the use case.

Why is this a problem from a test design standpoint? Consider the number of paths dictated by combinations of inputs where each input has ten possible values. As illustrated in Figure 5-2, as the number of inputs to be tested grows, the combinations of input values – and hence paths through the use case -- grows from the hundreds, to millions, to billions.

| # Inputs | Combinations | |
|---|---|---|
| 2 | 100 | |
| 3 | 1,000 | Thousands |
| 4 | 10,000 | |
| 5 | 100,000 | |
| 6 | 1,000,000 | Millions |
| 7 | 10,000,000 | |
| 8 | 100,000,000 | |
| 9 | 1,000,000,000 | Billions |
| 10 | 10,000,000,000 | |

Figure 5-2: Combinatorial explosion in number of paths through a use case

Neither a control flow graph or decision table approach is useful for tackling this type of problem. Take as an example, a use case involving making a call with a cell phone.[41] The use case involves three inputs / factors whose various combinations of values describe 18 potential scenarios of the use case to be tested ( 3 x 3 x 2 = 18 ):

- Call Type
  1) Free
  2) Chargeable National

---

[41] Example from Lloyd Roden, "Pairwise Testing", Better Software Magazine, October 2007

      3) Chargeable International
- Call Method
      1) Phone Book
      2) Voice Activated
      3) Quick Dial
- Account Type
      1) Pay As You Go
      2) Contract

All 18 combinations are indeed valid, but do we really need to test them all? If not, which? This is where pairwise testing is useful. Pairwise testing is *"a black box test design technique in which test cases are designed to execute all possible discrete combinations of each pair of input parameters"* [42]

The reasoning behind pairwise testing is the conventional wisdom that most failures are accounted for by things that fail on their own (single-mode faults, i.e. a single input), or as a result of the interaction of two-things (double-mode faults, i.e. two inputs). It is not to say there are not failures that result from the interaction of three or more factors, just that the probability of their happening becomes increasingly rare as the number of inputs / factors involved in the fault increases.

So by focusing test design on scenarios of the use case that exercise *only* pairs of inputs, we test for the most likely problems (single and double mode faults) plus we stand a good chance of stumbling onto some higher-mode faults just by accident!

*EXAMPLE*
There are three ways to approach pairwise test design. The first is the "low tech" approach. By this I simply mean to use this knowledge – pairwise test design is a "high bang for buck" way to approach combinations of inputs to the use case – as a heuristic to guide your otherwise manual test design. Don't try to cover all possible combinations of inputs; just focus on pairs.

---

[42] ISTQB Glossary

The second approach is what I call a "mid tech" approach. This involves what is known as *orthogonal arrays*. I call this approach "mid tech" because it does not necessarily rely on software support for test design (although having a computer with spreadsheet software or a word processor makes this approach a lot easier). But I think most testers already familiar with orthogonal arrays would agree describing their use is anything but "mid tech". Several good books and articles exist on the topic so I'll leave it to the reader to refer to those if interested in pursuing this approach.[43],[44],[45]

The third approach is the "high tech" approach, and this involves using a software tool to aid in test design. One such tool that is easy to use, readily available and free is "Allpairs". It's a simple tool -- compiled Perl script – distributed by testing consultant James Bach. No, it doesn't have some of the bells and whistles of high-dollar packages that are available, but did I mention it was free and easy to use?!

Let's return to our cell phone call use case and apply Allpairs to the problem of designing pair-wise tests.[46] The input to Allpairs is simply a tab limited text file ( see Figure 5-3). The first row provides the header for each column; these are the inputs / factors that characterize various scenarios of the use case, just like a decision table. Under each header is listed possible values for that input you want to test.

| Call Type | Call Method | Account Type |
|---|---|---|
| Free | Phone Book | Pay As You Go |
| Chargeable National | Voice Activated | Contract |
| Chargeable International | Quick Dial | |

Figure 5-3 Input to Allpairs is a tab delimited text file

---

[43] Rick Craig and Stefan Jaskiel, *Systematic Software Testing*, 2002
[44] Lee Copeland, *A Practitioner's Guide to Software Test Design*, 2004
[45] Roden, "Pairwise Testing".
[46] Roden works this example both using orthogonal arrays and with Allpairs providing a good comparison of the two approaches.

Once the input file is created, Allpairs is executed via simple command line prompt (Figure 5-4), providing it the input file (Figure 5-3), and the file in which you want the results placed.

```
C:\ Cmd
Microsoft Windows XP [Version 5.1.2600]
(C) Copyright 1985-2001 Microsoft Corp.

C:\>allpairs cellphone_inputs.txt > pairs_to_test.txt

C:\>
```

Figure 5-4 Allpairs is executed via simple command line prompt

Figure 5-5 shows the results produced by Allpairs.

| case | Call Type | Call Method | Account Type | pairings |
|------|-----------|-------------|--------------|----------|
| 1 | Free | Phone Book | Pay As You Go | 3 |
| 2 | Free | Voice Activated | Contract | 3 |
| 3 | Chargeable National | Phone Book | Contract | 3 |
| 4 | Chargeable National | Voice Activated | Pay As You Go | 3 |
| 5 | Chargeable International | Quick Dial | Pay As You Go | 3 |
| 6 | Chargeable International | Phone Book | Contract | 2 |
| 7 | Free | Quick Dial | Contract | 2 |
| 8 | Chargeable National | Quick Dial | ~Pay As You Go | 1 |
| 9 | Chargeable International | Voice Activated | ~Pay As You Go | 1 |

Figure 5-5 Results produced by Allpairs

The first column of Figure 5-5 is simply a number for that test case, in this case (applied to use cases) a particular scenario of the cell phone use case. The first thing to notice is that by focusing on just pairs of inputs – rather than all possible combinations of inputs – we've dropped the number of paths through the use case to be tested from eighteen to nine. While a 50% reduction in test cases is nothing to complain about, things get even better. The larger the input space, the larger the reduction you'll see over exhaustive test of all combinations of inputs. For the example of Figure 5-2 (illustrative of a use case with ten inputs) Bach says Allpairs can achieve all pairwise coverage of inputs in 177 cases. From billions of test cases to hundreds. Not bad.

The next three columns are the input pairings for each path.

The last column – "pairings" – shows how many unique pairings were accomplished in this case. This is a powerful tool for "working smart" in test design so let's talk about this a bit.

### WORKING SMART WITH PAIRWISE TESTING

As indicated by the last column, in case #1, we paired unique input values of Call Type with Call Method, Call Type with Account Type, and Call Method with Account Type. So a pairing of three input values. The same thing applies for cases #2-5; by adding each of those new test cases, we are able to accomplish three new pairings of input values.

Notice however that in cases #6 and 7 the number has dropped to two. This is reflecting a diminishing return on investment in adding more test cases. And by the time we get to cases #8 and 9 we are only exploring one new pairing for each test we add. So in a pinch for time in test design, the pairing column is a great guide for when the ROI on adding more tests is dropping off.

One last thing to mention about the Allpairs results that you as a test designer can leverage. The "~" symbol on input value Pay As You Go in cases #8 and 9 is Allpair's way of saying it has already paired all values of Account Type with every value for every other input so feel free to use whatever other value you want to use here. So if there's a particular value for Account Type you as a tester are most concerned about, you can substitute that value.

### FUN WITH ALLPAIRS: SANITY CHECKING A DECISION TABLE

Tools like Allpairs are (for geeks like me at least) just plain fun to play with. With a little imagination you'll find many applications. Here's one, a way to use Allpairs to help you as a tester think outside the box a little, generating ideas for tests you may have missed through other test design methods.

Recall our decision table from the previous section (Table 5-1) for describing the various scenarios of the **Do Book Search** use case; if pairwise testing is a good thing for helping find double-mode faults, a reasonable question a tester might ask in sanity checking a decision table is: Has the decision table addressed all valid pairs of inputs?

One could certainly check it manually (remember, the "low tech" approach to pairwise testing), but it's a lot more fun – and thorough – to let a tool like Allpairs help out. Figure 5-6 shows the input to Allpairs for the decision table. And Figure 5-7 shows the results.

| Login ID and Password | Curator | Librarian | Search Query |
|---|---|---|---|
| Valid | Yes | Yes | Found |
| Failed | No | No | Not Found |

Figure 5-6 Input to Allpairs for Do Book Search decision table

| case | Login ID and Password | Curator | Librarian | Search Query | pairings |
|---|---|---|---|---|---|
| 1 | Valid | Yes | Yes | Found | 6 |
| 2 | Valid | No | No | Not Found | 6 |
| 3 | Failed | Yes | No | Found | 5 |
| 4 | Failed | No | Yes | Not Found | 5 |
| 5 | ~Valid | Yes | ~Yes | Not Found | 1 |
| 6 | ~Valid | No | ~No | Found | 1 |

Figure 5-7 Results from Allpairs for the decision table

Inspecting the results in Figure 5-7 we notice first that cases #1, 2 and 6 are accounted for as-is in the decision table (Table 5-1) as scenarios #5, 2 and 1 respectively. But cases #3, 4 and 5 of Figure 5-7 are not accounted for in the decision table. Let's look at their pairings of inputs to see what we may have missed in the decision table that might be worth testing.

Allpairs' cases #3 and 4 illustrate one pairing (Login Id and Search Query) we assume should never happen, i.e. if the login fails, we naturally assume the user should not be able to proceed to execute a search. Allpairs is not a decision table generator (that would require domain specific knowledge) and has no feature for restricting certain combinations of inputs ( though some tools do; remember my comment about it not having all the bells and whistles of some commercial tools ). It simply does the brute force work of looking for all pairs of inputs. Still, presenting us with cases like this helps in challenging our assumptions.

Allpairs' cases #3 and 4 also bring up questions about the pairings of Login Id, Curator and Librarian. In our decision table (Table 5-1) we have a single scenario (#6) for testing failed login, i.e. if the user presents an invalid login ID and or password their login fails. But nowhere in the decision table do we test failure to login for IDs specifically associated with librarian, non-librarian, curator, or non-curator. Is there a possibility of a fault that allows, say, a librarian or curator to login despite a bogus password?

Finally, Allpairs' case #5 brings up a question about pairings of Login ID and Search Query. In the decision table the only failed search query tested is the one where the user is *neither* a curator or librarian (Table 5-1, scenario #2). Do we need tests that search queries correctly fail if the user is a librarian or curator?

These scenarios may or may not be ones we need to test for. The point being that a tool like Allpairs is easy enough to use that it comes in handy for helping you think outside the box about combinations of inputs that you may have missed.

## CHAPTER REVIEW

Let's review what we've covered.

In this, Part II of the book, we are focused on design of tests around paths through a single use case.

While control flow graphs have a lot going for them to address this level of test, it's good to have other testing tools in your tool box that work at this level. This chapter looked at two: decision tables and pairwise testing.

A decision table is a table showing combinations of inputs with their associated outputs and/or actions (effects). Notable applications of decision tables to use cases are Robert Binder's[47] Extended Use Case Test Design Pattern, and Leffingwell and Widrig's "test matrix" [48]

For some use cases the various paths through a use case are determined by inputs that are independent of each other: any combination of input values is valid, and results in a path through the use case, and the number of combinations can be prohibitive to test. For such use cases, pairwise testing is a good technique.

The reasoning behind pairwise testing is the conventional wisdom that most failures are accounted for by things that fail on their own (single-mode faults, i.e. a single input), or as a result of the interaction of two-things (double-mode faults, i.e. two inputs).

So by focusing test design on scenarios of the use case that exercise *only* pairs of inputs, we test for the most likely problems – single and double mode faults.

We concluded the discussion of pairwise testing by looking at the use of a simple tool -- compiled Perl script – distributed by testing consultant James Bach, and even looked at ways to use the tool as a sanity check on decision tables.

---

[47] Binder, *Testing Object-Oriented Systems*
[48] Leffingwell & Widrig, *Managing Software Requirements*

# PART III: SINGLE SCENARIO

## TEST DESIGN FROM 10,000 FEET

In this book we have been using the idea of use case levels of test as a way to organize how you approach test design. Each use case level of test comes with a set of test techniques that work well at that level. And each level of test provides a way to prioritize where you spend time in test design, the assumption being that you probably don't have time to write full blown tests for everything that needs to be tested (use cases being a good proxy test for parts of the system for which you don't get around to more formal test design; refer back to section Key Role of Use Cases in the Strategy).

In Part I of the book we approached test design from 30,000-foot level of test. This was test design at the system level as a whole as characterized by the use case diagram. At that level, paths through the system are in terms of traffic trod across a whole set of use cases, those belonging to the use case diagram.

In Part II we dropped to 20,000 feet and looked at test design for high priority use cases we identified at the 30,000-foot level. Test design at the 20,000-foot level was characterized as identifying the various paths through a use case, each path being a different scenario of the use case.

In this, Part III, we arrive at what I call the 10,000-foot view and test design will focus on a single scenario of a use case.

While a scenario represents a single path through the system from a black-box perspective, at the code level there's a pretty good chance that different inputs to the same scenario actually cause the code to execute different paths.

If we could peer under the hood at the code, we could re-apply techniques like control flow graphing to continue drilling down on finer granularity paths through the code itself, identifying tests for each. That's white-box testing, aka structural testing. There are reasons however to want to continue test design from a black box perspective. E.g. white-box testing is great for coverage of the code that's there – i.e.

faults of commission -- but what about faults of omission? Or maybe you are writing tests before the code is even written (a good way to find problems with the requirements). And last but not least, white-box testing is usually more practical for the development team that has access to the code and tools to help with code coverage measurement. For an independent test team dropping down to the code level is usually just not practical.

That brings us to test design from a scenario's inputs or outputs.

While a scenario represents a single path through the system, at the code level different inputs to the same scenario likely cause the code to execute differently, if only slightly. Chapter 6 looks at test design from scenario inputs in the hope that we are more fully testing the paths through the actual code, looking at the most widely discussed topics in input testing: error guessing, random input testing, equivalence partitioning, and boundary value analysis.

For a use case scenario with more than a single input, a good next step after selecting test inputs for each separate input is to look at *how to test the inputs in combination*. Chapter 6 concludes with ideas for "working smart" in striking the balance between rigor and practicality for testing inputs in combination.

Chapter 7 looks at additional techniques for describing inputs and how they are used to do equivalence partitioning and boundary value analysis testing.

Syntax diagrams will look very familiar as they re-use directed graphs, which you've already seen in control flow graphs. Regular expressions are cousins of syntax diagrams, though not graphic (visual) in nature. For the adventuresome at heart the last technique discussed in Chapter 7 is recursive definitions and will include examples written in Prolog (Programming in Logic).

## PRIORITIZING WHERE YOU DO INPUT TESTING

Before we dive into input testing, a reminder that you'll want to first begin by prioritizing which scenarios to focus on (Refer back to the prioritization strategy laid out back in Figure 0-4).

In Chapter 4 Use of Control Flow Graph in Load and Stress Testing, we discussed that just as some use cases receives more traffic than others, given a single use case, some paths – or scenarios – of the use case receive more traffic than others. The strategy for working smart at this point then is to apply input testing to the high traffic scenarios of the high traffic use cases.

# Chapter 6 TEST DESIGN FROM SCENARIO INPUTS

While a scenario represents a single path through the system, at the code level there's a pretty good chance that different inputs to the same scenario actually cause the code to execute differently, if only slightly.

If we could peer inside the black-box at the code, we could re-apply techniques like control flow graphing to continue drilling down on finer granularity paths through the code itself, identifying tests for each. That's white-box testing, aka structural testing. There are reasons however to want to continue test design from a black box perspective. For example white-box testing is great for coverage of the code that's there – i.e. faults of commission -- but what about faults of omission? Or maybe you are writing tests before the code is even written (a good way to find problems with the requirements). And last but not least, white-box testing is usually more practical for the development team that has access to the code and tools to help with code coverage measurement. For an independent test team dropping down to the code level is usually just not practical.

In this chapter we are going to look at black-box techniques for test design from scenario inputs (and they work for outputs also) in the hopes that we are more fully testing the paths through the actual code. In particular, we're going to ask a question few books do: does equivalence partitioning – arguably the most widely described technique for input testing -- really work?

## PRIORITIZING THE RIGOR OF TEST DESIGN

Let's begin with some ideas on how to prioritize where to apply the techniques in this chapter. First, recall that in Chapter 2, From Use Case Diagram to Operational Profile, we discussed the operational profile as a tool to spot the high traffic use cases of your system. Figure 2-8 from that chapter provided as an example how you might budget test design time at the use case level based on the operational profile. So scenarios of high traffic use cases probably deserve more input testing than scenarios of low traffic use cases.

Then in Chapter 4, Use of Control Flow Graph in Load and Stress Testing, we extended the notion of the operational profile to the individual paths or scenarios of a single use case. In that section we provided a "high-tech" approach using a control flow graph of the use case to spot the high traffic scenarios, and a "low-tech" approach using the Pareto principle.

Putting those two types of operational profiles together we have a heuristic for prioritizing which scenarios get lots of rigor: High traffic scenarios of high traffic use cases deserve more focus on test design from their inputs and outputs.

## A SIMPLE EXAMPLE TO START THINGS OFF

In a bit we'll be looking at test design from the inputs of the "happy path" scenario of the **Do Book Search** use case. But let's kick things off with a very easy use case scenario, but one that also helps make a number of points as we work through the example.

Figure 6-1 shows a very simple use case scenario for calculating tax for users with taxable income between $50,000 to $51,000. Table 6-1 then provides the specifics of the expected results for scenario step #3.

First point to make. As mentioned earlier, while a scenario is just a single path through the system, the code that underlines that single use case scenario may have a variety of paths through it. Imagine the code that implements the tax calculations described in Table 6-1. From a black-box testing perspective, we now rely on testing the inputs to explore those underlying paths in the code.

Second point. Again, as mentioned earlier, why not simply peer inside the black-box and design tests directly from the code? While we certainly could do that as a way of testing the various paths through the code, who is to say that what the code implements actually meets the requirements, in this case the tax calculations described by Table 6-1? It remains the job of black-box test design to implement tests of whether the code implements the required tax calculations.

Finally, this example is a great illustration of how use cases can be combined with alternate specification techniques – here a decision table -- to flesh out the bigger picture.

Now let's get on with our example of testing the inputs to this use case scenario.

## Use Case: **Calculate Tax Due**

Calculate tax due for users with taxable income between $50,000 to $51,000

## Main Scenario Steps

- User enters taxable income from line 43
- User selects filing status from pull-down
- System responds with tax due based on the 2010 Tax Table

Figure 6-1 Main scenario calculating tax due

**2010 Tax Table**–*Continued*

| If line 43 (taxable income) is— | | And you are— | | | |
|---|---|---|---|---|---|
| At least | But less than | Single | Married filing jointly | Married filing sepa-rately | Head of a house-hold |
| | | | Your tax is— | | |
| **50,000** | | | | | |
| 50,000 | 50,050 | 8,688 | 6,666 | 8,688 | 7,354 |
| 50,050 | 50,100 | 8,700 | 6,674 | 8,700 | 7,366 |
| 50,100 | 50,150 | 8,713 | 6,681 | 8,713 | 7,379 |
| 50,150 | 50,200 | 8,725 | 6,689 | 8,725 | 7,391 |
| 50,200 | 50,250 | 8,738 | 6,696 | 8,738 | 7,404 |
| 50,250 | 50,300 | 8,750 | 6,704 | 8,750 | 7,416 |
| 50,300 | 50,350 | 8,763 | 6,711 | 8,763 | 7,429 |
| 50,350 | 50,400 | 8,775 | 6,719 | 8,775 | 7,441 |
| 50,400 | 50,450 | 8,788 | 6,726 | 8,788 | 7,454 |
| 50,450 | 50,500 | 8,800 | 6,734 | 8,800 | 7,466 |
| 50,500 | 50,550 | 8,813 | 6,741 | 8,813 | 7,479 |
| 50,550 | 50,600 | 8,825 | 6,749 | 8,825 | 7,491 |
| 50,600 | 50,650 | 8,838 | 6,756 | 8,838 | 7,504 |
| 50,650 | 50,700 | 8,850 | 6,764 | 8,850 | 7,516 |
| 50,700 | 50,750 | 8,863 | 6,771 | 8,863 | 7,529 |
| 50,750 | 50,800 | 8,875 | 6,779 | 8,875 | 7,541 |
| 50,800 | 50,850 | 8,888 | 6,786 | 8,888 | 7,554 |
| 50,850 | 50,900 | 8,900 | 6,794 | 8,900 | 7,566 |
| 50,900 | 50,950 | 8,913 | 6,801 | 8,913 | 7,579 |
| 50,950 | 51,000 | 8,925 | 6,809 | 8,925 | 7,591 |

Table 6-1 Tax Table for 2010

## DEFINE THE DOMAIN OF EACH INPUT

In testing, a domain is *"the set from which valid input and/or output values can be selected"* [49],[50] It comes from the mathematical use of the term in set theory referring to the set of values that a function (or more generally a relation) takes as inputs. It's not to be confused with other uses of the term "domain", as in say application domain (e.g. banking), or internet domain. And to make it even more confusing, in testing lingo the term "domain" is applied to both inputs and outputs, while in set theory the latter is called the range.

The first step in nearly all test design from inputs is to "simply" define the domain of the input. I put "simply" in quotes because as we'll see as we progress through the chapter, defining the domain is the hardest part. Once done, the rest is a piece of cake!

In our example, we have two inputs to the scenario: Taxable Income and Filing Status. The valid inputs for each are:

- Taxable Income : $50,000 – $50,999.99[51]
- Filing Status : { Single, Married filing jointly, Married filing separately, Head of a household }

That was easy! Why bother doing this? If we do no more than this for a scenario, it provides a tester a basis (even if subconsciously) for error guessing, and is usually a necessary step for all the other techniques we'll discuss.

------

[49] ISTQB Glossary
[50] In discrete math, the term "range" is standard nomenclature for the set of all possible values of the output of a function or binary relation. It's the same concept as the "domain" of an input, but applies to the output instead. In testing lingo, this distinction is not always made and the term "domain" may be applied to the output as well as input.
[51] The tax table says *less* than 51,000

## ERROR GUESSING

Error guessing is *"A test design technique where the experience of the tester is used to anticipate what defects might be present in the component or system under test as a result of errors made, and to design tests specifically to expose them"*[52]

An application generic form of error guessing is selecting values at extremes of the domain of an input, or values outside the domain of an input (invalid inputs). This is the basis for boundary value analysis which we'll discuss shortly. An application specific error guess for our tax example might be, say (and this is totally contrived), that taxable incomes with a "9" seem to historically cause errors due to rounding errors.

## RANDOM INPUT TESTING

Random testing is *"A black box test design technique where test cases are selected, possibly using a pseudo-random generation algorithm, to match an operational profile"*[53]

A few things worth noting about this definition to understand what is really implied by random input testing. First point is about the verbiage "random generation algorithm": this type of testing is meant to be – well, *random* – as opposed to error guessing which is intended to be biased (even if unconsciously) by the experience / background of the tester. Nor is there any formal test design (one might construe error guessing as informal test design) behind random input testing: if you design tests they are of course not random.

The idea is that through random selection of inputs, you will "stumble on" errors that you might otherwise overlook. Random input testing works best with applications where automated testing is possible and inputs can be generated by some sort of automated random input generation tool, but can be done with manual test execution if there's some way to randomize input selection.

---

[52] ISTQB Glossary
[53] ISTQB Glossary

A second point is the verbiage about "operational profile": in order for randomness to stumble-onto errors, you will probably need to allocate test time in proportion to anticipated frequency of use by the user, i.e. by an operational profile. Recall in Figure 2-8 where we used the operational profile to budget 20 hours of test design? The same idea works for random input testing, but rather than budgeting time for test design we budget time to conduct random input testing.

## EQUIVALENCE PARTITIONING

There is perhaps no other topic in software testing that has been discussed as much as equivalence partitions (also called equivalence classes). The first book I'm aware of that included a discussion of equivalence partitioning was Glenford Myer's[54]. Virtually every book since then on software testing – or that includes a discussion of software testing – has discussed the topic. Given the exposure we test practitioners receive to the topic – books, classes, certification exams (e.g. ISTBQ), classes, conference presentations, etc.. – it's interesting how little is ever mentioned of the debates in the testing research community as to whether equivalence partitioning is really effective (it finds bugs) or efficient (it finds bugs at a low cost compared to say random input testing).

So in this section, let's start with a quick explanation on the topic (on the off chance you have not yet encountered this technique) then review some of the research that has transpired looking at effectiveness and efficiency of the technique. We'll conclude the section with lessons learned from the research on how to best use equivalence partitioning.

### WHAT IS IT?

An equivalence class or partition is *"A portion of an input or output domain for which the behavior of a component or system is assumed to be the same, based on the specification".* Equivalence partitioning is *"A black box test design technique in which test cases are designed to execute representatives from equivalence partitions. In principle test cases are designed to cover each partition at least once".*[55]

---

[54] Glenford Myers, *The Art of Software Testing*, John Wiley & Sons, 1979
[55] ISTQB Glossary

The motivation for equivalence partitioning is that, practically speaking, the domain of an input is usually so large that we can't test every value. So wouldn't it be great to be able to divide the input space into non-overlapping partitions such that we could select just one test case from each partition such that – quoting Myers -- *"one can reasonably assume (but, of course, not be absolutely sure) that a test of a representative value of each class is equivalent to a test of any other value. That is, if one test case in an equivalence class detects an error, all other test cases in the equivalence class would be expected to find the same error. Conversely, if a test case did not detect an error, we would expect that no other test cases in the equivalence class would find an error (unless a subset of the equivalence class falls within another equivalence class, since equivalence classes may overlap one another)".*

Using our tax example of Table 6-1 the taxable income we are testing has a domain of from $50,000.00 to $50,999.99. That's an input space of 99,900 possible inputs: 999 integers representing the dollar amounts from $50,000 to $50,999 (one penny less than $51,000); and 100 integers representing the cents from 0 to 99 cents.

That is, of course, a lot of inputs to test. But as it turns out, there is a straightforward way to partition the input space, that is by tax bracket, i.e. by rows of the table. Since each row of the tax table represents an income tax bracket , it's reasonable to assume that if the tax calculation for one value of a row is in error, then the tax calculation for other incomes in that bracket will be in error as well. Similarly, if the tax calculation is correct, the tax calculation for other incomes in that bracket will probably be correct as well. To be sure, not all input domains are this straightforward to partition as we'll see later ( Chapter 7Advanced Techniques for Input Testing).

By testing one input from each tax bracket of the table – i.e. each row – we've reduced the number of inputs to test from 99,900 down to 20! Quite a savings in test effort.

An important point to be made is there is usually more than one way to "slice and dice" the input space. Here's a simple example. Say one of the inputs to a use case scenario is an integer that ranges from -200 through +200.

One set of equivalence partitions for the input space might be the following, using the criterion of the sign of the number:

- -200 to -1 (negative sign)
- 0 (no sign)
- 1 to 200 (positive sign)

Another way to partition the input space might be using the criterion of the number of digits in the input:

- Values with one digit (e.g., -9, 0, 1)
- Values with two digits (e.g., -99, 11, 99)
- Values with three digits (e.g., -200, 100, 200)

Finally, equivalence partitioning is an appropriate technique not only for valid inputs, but also for invalid inputs.

In our tax example, for this specific table, the taxable income we are testing has a domain of from $50,000.00 to $50,999.99. This provides two obvious equivalence partitions of invalid entries, namely values less than $50,000.00, and values greater than $50,999.99. The former partition might be further partitioned, into say negative, zero and positive values less than $50,000.00.

The application of equivalence partitioning to outputs is less common, but works like this: the output space (valid or invalid) is partitioned, then an output from each partition selected as a target so to speak, one then determines an appropriate input that would cause that output to be generated.

While equivalence partitioning certainly is one of the most discussed topics in the testing literature, there are some (potential) skeletons in the closet, which surprisingly have gotten little mention in popular books on testing. Let's take a look at two.

## LETTER OF THE LAW VS. SPIRIT OF THE LAW

Numeric examples of equivalence partitions are the most commonly cited. For one thing they are very easy to explain; and secondly, they produce true partitions. The "official party line" on equivalence partitioning is that when you partition the input space of an input, it produces partitions, that is to say a collection of mutually *non-overlapping* (disjoint) subsets, which collectively (the union of which) cover the entire input space. The official view is presented in any number of good books [56],[57] and is re-enforced by a wealth of examples, mostly numeric, like my tax example presented earlier.

But practically speaking – i.e. in the real world where pressure is on to get tests designed – a tester may wind up with partitions that do in fact overlap, which in some cases can be fixed by careful (read more time spent in analysis ) reconsideration of the criterion used.

That particular case aside (you wind up with partitions that overlap due to "poor choice" of partitioning criterion) one skeleton in the testing research communities closet is that some very valid "partitioning" techniques don't always partition the input in this strict sense of partitioning.

To quote from a paper by Weyuker and Jeng[58], *"The term 'partition testing,' in its broadest sense, refers to a very general family of testing strategies. The primary characteristic is that the program's input domain is divided into subsets, with the tester selecting one or more element from each subdomain. In the testing literature, it is common not to restrict the term 'partition' to the formal mathematical meaning of a division into disjoint subsets, which together span the space being considered. Instead, testers generally use it in the more informal sense to refer to a division into (possibly overlapping) subsets of the domain. The goal of such a partitioning is to make the division in such a way that when the tester selects test cases based on the subsets, the resulting test set is a good representation of the entire domain."*

So I think it's important for the working tester to realize when it comes to input partitioning, there's the letter of the law, but then there's the spirit of the law being referred to by Weyuker and Jeng, and it's possible to achieve the latter while violating the former.

---

[56] Jorgensen, Software Testing
[57] Aditya P. Mathur, *Foundations of Software Testing*, 2008
[58] Elaine J. Weyuker and Bingchiang Jeng, "Analyzing Partition Testing Strategies", *IEEE TRANSACTIONS ON SOFIWARE ENGINEERING*, VOL. 17, NO. 7, JULY 1991

## DOES EQUIVALENCE PARTITIONING REALLY WORK?

As the tax example illustrates, equivalence partitioning can drastically reduce the input space to be tested. But does it work? As previously mentioned, given the coverage the topic of equivalence partitioning has received, it's surprising so little is mentioned in the popular literature about the debates in the research community as to whether it's really an effective and efficient test strategy. This is our second skeleton in the closet of equivalence partitioning.

In the 70s, test experts tended to doubt the efficiency of random input testing. Myer's book first published in 1979 -- one of the first to address equivalence partitioning – said, for example *"probably the poorest [testing] methodology of all is random-input testing – the process of testing a program by selecting, at random, some subset of all possible input values.* Myers then proceeded to explain that what the tester needed were techniques that *"allow one to select a set of test data more intelligently"*, one of those (for black-box testing) being *equivalence partitioning.*

In 1984 two researches -- J.W. Duran and S.C. Ntafos[59] -- published a paper that started questioning this assumption. Although the paper was a defense of random input testing, an alternative interpretation was not so much that random input testing wasn't so bad, but rather, equivalence partitioning may not really be all that good. And the kicker of course was that equivalence partitioning usually requires a larger effort in terms of analysis, i.e. the effort required to actually figure out how to best partition the input domain into equivalence partitions.

This paper kicked off a debate on the topic of the effectiveness and efficiency of equivalence partitioning that was to span the next two decades. In 1990 Hamlet and Taylor, at first skeptical of the Duran and Ntafos results, published their own work basically confirming what Duran and Ntafos had found; the title of one of their papers pretty much says it all: *"Partition Testing Does Not Inspire Confidence".* [60]

---

[59] J.W. Duran and S.C. Ntafos, "An Evaluation of Random Testing" *IEEE Trans. Software Eng.*, vol. 10, pp. 438–444, 1984.

[60] R. Hamlet and R. Taylor, "Partition Testing Does Not Inspire Confidence," *IEEE Trans. Software Eng.*, vol. 16, pp. 1,402–1,411, 1990.

In 1991 Weyuker and Jeng then published a paper[61] -- quoting Gutjahr[62] -- *".. that compared the two testing approaches [finding] a clear superiority of partition testing could not be stated (emphasis mine); instead, it turned out that, in effectiveness, partition testing can be better, worse or the same as random testing .. depending on the "adequacy" of the chosen partition with respect to the location of the failure-causing inputs".* Remember in the previous section that an input space can usually be partitioned in more than one way. The problem being pointed out here is that the effectiveness of the technique rests upon the partitioning chosen, but how to know which to choose?

By the late 90s / early 2000s however, the pendulum had partly begun to swing back, if not fully endorsing equivalence partitioning, at least qualifying the previously published negative findings. Gutjahr's paper from 1999 concluded, in brief, *"..in spite of (erroneous) conclusions that might possibly be drawn from previous investigations, partition–based testing techniques are well-founded.." (again, emphasis mine).*

And Ntafos, one of the authors of the original 1984 paper that kicked off the debate, published a paper in 2001[63] also citing problems with previous studies and concluded that *"Comparisons that use practical metrics and involve actual testing strategies... are needed to better illuminate the random versus partition testing question".* In other words, it depends a bit on how you define (and hence measure) effectiveness or efficiency to say whether equivalence partitioning is better or worse than, say, random input testing.

That dialogue spanning 20 years certainly gives the tester in the work a day world reason to reflect: To partition, or not to partition: That is the question!

---

[61] E.J. Weyuker and B. Jeng, "Analyzing Partition Testing Strategies," *IEEE Trans. Software Eng.*, vol. 17, pp. 703–711, 1991.
[62] Walter J. Gutjahr, Partition Testing vs. Random Testing: The Influence of Uncertainty, *IEEE Transactions on Software Engineering archive*, Volume 25 Issue 5, September 1999
[63] Simeon C. Ntafos, On Comparisons of Random, Partition, and Proportional Partition Testing, *IEEE TRANSACTIONS ON SOFTWARE ENGINEERING*, VOL. 27, NO. 10, OCTOBER 2001

What lessons learned are to be had from all this research. As a non-researcher, my take-aways as they pertain to the subject of this book – use case driven test design – are:

- Equivalence partitioning is most appropriately used to test the inputs at the *scenario* level. This is opposed e.g. to relying on it to test the various paths through a use case by partitioning the inputs to the use case as a whole.
- Because there is no one way to partition the input, and the "effectiveness" of the technique seems to hinge in large part on the partitioning strategy used, if you are dealing with a scenario that requires more rigor in test design, you might do well to partition the input in more than a single way and/or combine it with another input testing strategy, e.g. random input testing or error guessing.
- And finally .. see Boundary Value Analysis next!

## BOUNDARY VALUE ANALYSIS

While in theory all the elements of an equivalence partition are equivalent (hence the name), in practice, conventional wisdom holds that bugs more often lurk at the boundaries of the equivalence partitions.

Boundary value analysis (also called boundary value testing) is *"A black box test design technique in which test cases are designed based on boundary values"*. A boundary value is *"An input value or output value which is on the edge of an equivalence partition or at the smallest incremental distance on either side of an edge, for example the minimum or maximum value of a range."* [64]

And the conventional wisdom seems to be backed by research. One example, a paper by Stuart Reid[65] in 1997 described the results of a case study based on an operational avionics system of approximately 20,000 lines of Ada code. The case study compared the effectiveness of not only equivalence partitioning (EP) and random input testing, but also boundary value analysis (BVA), concluding that ".."

---

[64] ISTQB Glossary
[65] Stuart C. Reid, "An empirical analysis of equivalence partitioning, boundary value analysis and random testing", *Proceedings of the Fourth Int'l Software Metrics Symposium, 1997*

126

*BVA was found to be most effective, with neither EP nor random testing half as effective.."*

Returning to our tax example, we previously partitioned the valid input domain of taxable income into 20 partitions, i.e. each row of Table 6-1 was considered an equivalence partition. Rather than arbitrarily choosing one test input for each row (per standard equivalence partitioning they are all equivalent, so arbitrary selection is possible), boundary value testing calls for us taking inputs at the boundaries. So for the first row of the table, we would test inputs of $50,000 and $50,049.99[66] and for the second row we would test $50,050 and $50,099.99.

Applying boundary value testing to each of the 20 rows of the table will result in 40 tests. Double the testing over straight equivalence partition testing. If in addition we follow the strategy sometimes taught with boundary value testing – pick an input at each boundary, *plus* one in the middle away from the boundaries – the number of tests would rise to 3 per row, or 60 overall.[67]

Because of the apparent effectiveness of boundary value testing, and because equivalence partitioning is the first necessary step towards identifying those boundaries, the two are sometimes presented as a single test design strategy. But just keep in mind, they are distinct, and in a pinch for time equivalence partition testing can be used separately from boundary value testing or used creatively with boundary value testing. For example, for half the rows of the tax table one might decide to select a single input arbitrarily selected midway *between* the boundaries, while for the other rows inputs at the boundaries are selected. This would result in 10 + 10*2 = 30 inputs to test.

Finally, boundary value testing applies to invalid inputs as well as valid. If invalid inputs for our tax table are values less than $50,000.00, and values greater than $50,999.99, boundary values would be $49,999.99 and $51,000.00 respectively.

---

[66] One penny less than $50,050
[67] Rick Craig and Stefan Jaskiel, *Systematic Software Testing*

## TESTING INPUTS IN COMBINATION

To this point we've talked about how to select values to test for a single input, e.g. by error guessing or use of a more systematic approach such as boundary value analysis.

For a use case scenario with more than a single input, the next question is how to test the inputs in combination. The answer to this needs to be broken into two categories. First, for tests of invalid inputs, the conventional wisdom is that invalid inputs be tested one at a time, that is *not* tested in combination so that one failure does not mask another.[68]

With that easy answer out of the way we turn to the more complicated question: testing *valid* inputs in combination. A paper by Grindall, Offutt and Andler [69] surveyed 16 different strategies for testing inputs in combination, covered in nearly 40 papers over two decades. In other words, there's no simple, hard and fast rule for this.

While the combination strategies are typically couched in terms of combinations of values selected from equivalence partitions, the three we'll look at work for any strategy for selecting values for each input, be it error guessing, equivalence partitioning, or boundary value testing ( if you are doing random input testing, combination testing of inputs is covered by random input selection ).

Recall that for our tax example of Table 6-1, we identified two inputs to the scenario: Taxable Income and Filing Status. And to recap, we identified the valid domain of each input as follows:

- Taxable Income : $50,000 – $50,999.99

---

[68] Myer's *Art of Software Testing*, John Wiley & Sons, 1979, was the first book I'm aware of to suggest this strategy and has been repeated in any number of books since.
[69] Grindal, M, Offutt, J, and Andler, S. F. (2005) Combination Testing Strategies: (A) Survey, publisher Wiley, Software Testing, Verification, and Reliability, volume 15, number 2, pp. 167-199.

- Filing Status : { Single, Married filing jointly, Married filing separately, Head of a household }

And as previously noted, Taxable Income can be partitioned by the rows of the tax table each row being an equivalence partition; so there are 20 equivalence partitions. The input Filing Status we have not partitioned yet. Unfortunately, since the tax computation for each of these statuses is different, they really all need to be tested. We can indeed partition the input into four equivalence classes, but each class would have just one element. So while by the "letter of the law" we can indeed partition this input, by the "spirit of the law" there's not much point: partitioning doesn't reduce the number of inputs to be tested (as an aside, this is usually the case with inputs that in statistics are called nominal, or categorical).

Now let's look at some strategies for how to test these inputs in combination, such that based on how much time you have to spend on test design – and subsequent test execution of those tests – you can ramp up the rigor from lower to higher.

### FEWEST TESTS NEEDED; LOWEST RIGOR

Let's assume that for Taxable Income we've decided to use boundary value analysis to identify the values to be tested for that input, selecting two values – the lowest and highest taxable income -- per equivalence partition. That results in 40 inputs to be tested: 20 equivalence partitions times 2 values per each. The second input, Filing Status, has four input values to be tested.

The combination strategy that uses the least number of tests is to produce just enough test cases that each value for each input appears at least once in a test case. Offutt and Ammann[70] refer to this as *each choice coverage*; Grindall, Offutt and Andler [71] refer to this as *each-used or 1-wise coverage* (as opposed to pair-wise or 2-wise, 3-wise, etc..); and Jorgen refers to this strategy as part of both *traditional equivalence class testing* and *weak equivalence class testing*.[72]

---

[70] Ammann and Offutt, *Introduction to Software Testing*
[71] Grindal, M, Offutt, J, and Andler, S. F. (2005) Combination Testing Strategies: (A) Survey, publisher Wiley, Software Testing, Verification, and Reliability, volume 15, number 2, pp. 167-199.
[72] Jorgensen, *Software Testing*

The number of test cases needed will always be the largest input space to be tested, in this case 40. Combining the 40 input values of Taxable Income with the four inputs for Filing Status, we might arrive at the combinations shown in Table 6-2.

Notice that once the four values of Filing Status have been tried at least once, you are at liberty to then repeat values as you see fit, e.g. combining various filing status with incomes based on error guessing.

| Taxable Income | Filing Status |
|---|---|
| $ 50,000.00 | Single |
| $ 50,049.99 | Married filing jointly |
| $ 50,050.00 | Married filing separately |
| $ 50,099.99 | Head of a household |
| $ 50,100.00 | Single |
| $ 50,149.99 | Married filing jointly |
| $ 50,150.00 | Married filing separately |
| $ 50,199.99 | Head of a household |
| $ 50,200.00 | Single |
| $ 50,249.99 | Married filing jointly |
| $ 50,250.00 | Married filing separately |
| $ 50,299.99 | Head of a household |
| $ 50,300.00 | Single |
| $ 50,349.99 | Married filing jointly |
| $ 50,350.00 | Married filing separately |
| $ 50,399.99 | Head of a household |
| $ 50,400.00 | Single |
| $ 50,449.99 | Married filing jointly |
| $ 50,450.00 | Married filing separately |
| $ 50,499.99 | Head of a household |
| $ 50,500.00 | Single |
| $ 50,549.99 | Married filing jointly |
| $ 50,550.00 | Married filing separately |
| $ 50,599.99 | Head of a household |
| $ 50,600.00 | Single |
| $ 50,649.99 | Married filing jointly |
| $ 50,650.00 | Married filing separately |
| $ 50,699.99 | Head of a household |
| $ 50,700.00 | Single |
| $ 50,749.99 | Married filing jointly |
| $ 50,750.00 | Married filing separately |
| $ 50,799.99 | Head of a household |
| $ 50,800.00 | Single |
| $ 50,849.99 | Married filing jointly |
| $ 50,850.00 | Married filing separately |
| $ 50,899.99 | Head of a household |
| $ 50,900.00 | Single |
| $ 50,949.99 | Married filing jointly |
| $ 50,950.00 | Married filing separately |
| $ 50,999.99 | Head of a household |

Table 6-2 Each input value to be tested appears in at least one test case

## GREATEST NUMBER OF TESTS; HIGHEST RIGOR

At the other end of the spectrum is a strategy that produces the most number of tests. It calls for taking all possible combinations of values across all the inputs. Ammann and Offutt call this appropriately *all combinations coverage*; this strategy is used in what Jorgen's calls *strong equivalence class testing*.

Combining the 40 input values of Taxable Income with the four inputs for Filing Status, results in 160 possible combinations. When using this approach, the tester may find that some combinations of inputs are not valid, in which case those combinations become candidate error tests.

## GOOD COMPROMISE ON NUMBER OF TESTS

For any use case scenario with more than 2 inputs, testing all combinations of input values may simply not be practical. And at the same time, 1-wise coverage may result in too few combinations tested. A happy compromise is do pairwise testing of the inputs. And the good news, you've already seen how to use this technique in Chapter 5, including the use of a free, readily available, easy to use tool: Allpairs.

Do keep in mind if using a tool such as Allpairs to help generate the pairwise combinations of inputs, there may be combinations that are not valid, and these are candidates for error tests: Tests that the application either prevents the user from entering those combinations, or if possible to enter them, the application has proper error handling for those combinations.

## CONCLUDING THOUGHTS: WORKING SMART IN COMBINATION TESTING

As previously mentioned, the paper by Grindall, Offutt and Andler surveying 16 different strategies in nearly 40 papers is a good illustration that there is no one right answer to how to test inputs in combination.

I think with creative use of the three techniques presented here (1-wise coverage, pairwise coverage, all combinations coverage) the working tester will have plenty to utilize. What do I mean by "creative"? It's easy when reading the literature to fall into a mindset of this technique, versus that technique, never the twain to meet. Remember, there's no rule that says you have to use one and only one technique at a time!

So being creative, say you have a scenario with 6 inputs. Through error guessing you identify the top three inputs you are concerned most with, do all combination or pairwise testing on those, then use 1-wise coverage for the remaining three inputs.

Finally, tools such as Allpairs which are based on "blind" combinations of values, are, I believe, still very useful even when there are combinations of values that aren't valid. As noted, these combinations are still candidate error tests, and I think it's less error prone for the tester to reject unwanted combinations than have to think of all possible combinations that may need testing ("Wow, I would have never thought of *that* combination of inputs!"). Even for scenarios of two inputs, I think it's worthwhile to use a tool like Allpairs.[73]

## CHAPTER REVIEW

Here's a recap of what we looked at in this chapter.

While a scenario represents a single path through the system, at the code level different inputs to the same scenario likely cause the code to execute differently, if only slightly. This chapter looked at test design from scenario inputs (and outputs) in the hope that we are more fully testing the paths through the actual code

In terms of prioritizing where these techniques are applied, high traffic scenarios of high traffic use cases deserve more focus on test design from their inputs and outputs.

The first step in nearly all test design from inputs is to define the domain of the input, the set from which valid (and conversely invalid) values can be selected.

Once the domain of an input is defined, one strategy for selecting test inputs is error guessing in which the experience of the tester is used to anticipate which inputs will result in failure.

---

[73] Pairwise testing of two inputs is equivalent to all combinations in terms of the number of tests needed.

Random testing of inputs involves the random selection of test inputs. Error guessing is *not* random testing. Error guessing is *intended* to be biased (even if unconsciously) by the experience / background of the tester. True random testing is meant to be truly random to "stumble on" errors that you might otherwise overlook.

The motivation for equivalence partitioning is that the domain of an input is usually so large that we can't test every value. Equivalence partitioning divides the input space into partitions such that all inputs from a given partition are thought to be equivalent in terms of finding defects, hence we simply test one input from each partition.

While in theory all the elements of an equivalence partition are equivalent, conventional wisdom holds that bugs frequent the *boundaries* of the equivalence partitions. Accordingly, boundary value analysis or boundary value testing is a test input selection strategy that calls for selecting test inputs at the boundaries of the equivalence partitions.

Techniques for selecting valid inputs to test, e.g. equivalence partitioning and boundary value analysis, work for selecting invalid inputs as well.

For a use case scenario with more than a single input, a good next step after selecting test inputs for each is to look at *how to test the inputs in combination*. For invalid inputs, the conventional wisdom is to test each one at a time, that is *not* tested in combination so that one failure does not mask another. For testing valid inputs in combination various strategies are available depending on how many tests you are willing to conduct. Ideas for "working smart" in striking the balance between rigor and practicality were discussed.

# Chapter 7 ADVANCED TECHNIQUES FOR INPUT TESTING

As mentioned in the last chapter, it's probably the case that no other topic in testing has been written about as much as equivalence partitioning and boundary value analysis. And it's also probably the case that virtually everyone uses a simple scalar, numeric input to explain equivalence partitioning and boundary value analysis, like my earlier example of an input that is an integer ranging from -200 through +200, or the tax example.

Wouldn't the tester's life be great if all inputs were this straightforward to partition! Alas, they are not. In this chapter we look at some additional techniques for describing inputs and how to do equivalence partitioning and boundary value analysis of the inputs based on those descriptions.

The three techniques we'll look at here come under the category of discrete math for testers and are more advanced tools for describing (modeling) inputs as a basis for equivalence partitioning and boundary value testing.

First are syntax diagrams which will look very familiar as they re-use directed graphs, which you've already seen in control flow graphs. Next we look at regular expressions, cousins of syntax diagrams, though not graphic (visual) in nature. Lastly we'll look at recursive definitions which define an input as one or more base cases and recursive rules. Recursive definitions are a powerful technique for describing inputs be they numeric in nature, sets of things, Boolean or syntactic.

## SYNTAX DIAGRAMS

It's always great when we can re-use something we already know how to use, and directed graphs are one of those "Swiss army knife" type techniques that can be used and re-used.

Back in Chapter 3 we used a directed graph to build a state transition diagram to show the allowed *sequence* of states in a data entity's lifecycle. Then in Chapter 4 we saw directed graphs used as a control flow graph, a tool for describing the various paths through a use case. Another way to think about that is that a path is a particular *sequence* of steps, or blocks of steps, in the use case. So it shouldn't be surprising to find that a directed graph can also be used to describe the allowed *sequence of characters* for an input; i.e. the input's syntax.

Remember the basic flow of our library **Do Book Search** use case (refer back to Figure 4-1)? The first step of that scenario involves the user logging into the system with an ID.

A natural language description of that ID might be, say, *"The user ID is a name, using upper or lower case letters, possibly hyphenated to allow for possible hyphenated surnames, with an optional number at the end to distinguish multiple persons with the same name".*

What we'd like to do is to write a description of all possible inputs that match that criteria, and in such a way that supports equivalence partitioning and boundary value analysis. One way to tackle that problem is to define the input with a syntax diagram, like that shown in Figure 7-1.[74],[75]

---

[74] See Niklaus Wirth, *Algorithms + Data Structures = Programs, Prentice-Hall, 1976* for an early application defining the syntax of the programming language Pascal. See Beizer, *Software Testing Techniques*, section Syntax Testing for a testing slant. Beizer calls them Syntax Graphs.
[75] "Full blown" syntax diagrams allow for recursion. We're going to restrict the discussion here to syntax diagrams without recursion, and talk about recursion in the last section of this chapter.

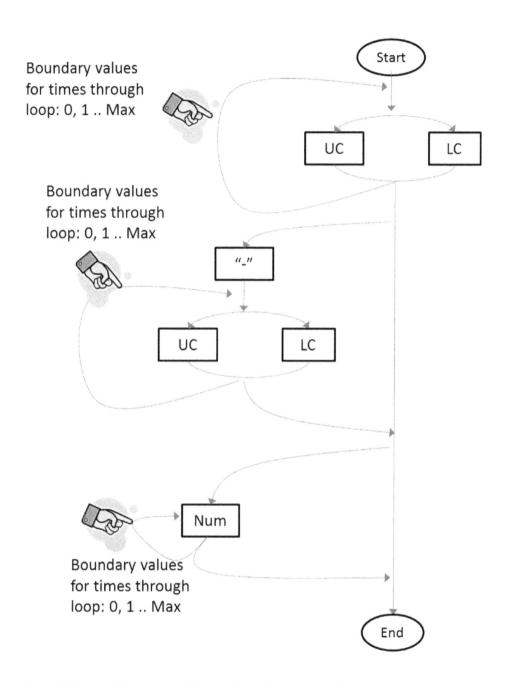

Boundary values for times through loop: 0, 1 .. Max

Boundary values for times through loop: 0, 1 .. Max

Boundary values for times through loop: 0, 1 .. Max

Start

UC    LC

"_"

UC    LC

Num

End

Figure 7-1 Syntax diagram of *valid* user login ID to Do Book Search use case

137

In a syntax diagram, nodes are used to indicate a character or token (a grouping of characters that form a larger unit of syntax, e.g. a variable name). Paths through the graph show the allowed sequence of characters or tokens.

In this graph the node labeled LC stands for any lower-case letter, e.g. "a", "b", "c" and so on. The node UC stands for any upper-case letter, e.g. "A", "B", "C" and so on. The node NUM stands any single digit, 0 through 9. And finally, the node labeled "-" stands for the hyphen. Any path through the graph from start to end defines a valid input for the user login ID.

## *EQUIVALENCE CLASSES*

A reasonable question at this point is that given the effort it requires to build a syntax diagram, what's the advantage over the natural language description? *i.e. "The user ID is a name, using upper or lower case letters, possibly hyphenated to allow for possible hyphenated surnames, with an optional number at the end".*

The answer is that by describing the input as a syntax diagram, we've done the hard work in identifying equivalence classes and boundary value tests. Each path through the graph is an equivalence class, or to quote Beizer "When we say .. that it is sufficient to test one set of input values for each [path] .. we are asserting that the set of all input values for each path .. is an equivalence class .."[76].

And we can reuse all the techniques from Chapter 4, Control Flow Graphs: Adjusting the Rigor of Test Design, to decide how much rigor – i.e. how many equivalence classes, and hence how many tests – we want to partition the input space into: node coverage, edge coverage, basis path coverage, or even all paths coverage if that is feasible.

Also as discussed in Chapter 4, we can quickly estimate the number of tests we are going to need by calculating the cyclomatic complexity: counting the regions (seven) of the graph and adding one, we get eight. So right away we know that we'll need *no more than* 8 for node or edge coverage, *exactly* eight for basis path coverage, and at *least* 8 if we deemed it important to shoot for all path coverage.

---

[76] Beizer, *Software Testing Techniques*, pg. 405

*BOUNDARY VALUE TESTS*

OK, so a path through the syntax diagram is an equivalence class. What about boundary value tests?

Boundary value testing comes into play in terms of the number of times a test executes a loop of a syntax diagram. I like to think of it in terms of two equivalence classes: zero times (the loop is skipped), and all other values greater than zero (the loop is not skipped). Zero times through the loop is an equivalence class with just a single element, so the boundary case there is zero. For the equivalence class of values greater than zero, the boundary cases are 1 and some max value.

So the boundary values of a loop are zero, once and some max.

The max values for a loop should be identified preferably via the requirements, e.g. how many characters / numbers does the requirement say we are to allow for each part of the user login ID, or collectively as a whole?

A couple of side notes on loop testing are in order. Beizer argues loops be tested zero, once, twice, a "typical" number of times and max times (and some of these cases may overlap). The motivation for the typical test is that "*if you [the tester] don't do it, your testing is sure to be criticized*". It is, as Beizer puts it, "*politically wise*". [77]

Also, Huang[78] makes a case for always testing a loop zero times, and two or more times, i.e. never *just* once. Certain "dataflow anomalies" will be found only if the loop is bypassed completely ( zero times through loop), and if the loop is iterated through two or more times. While the problem is motivated by loops at the coding level, because loops in syntax may mirror code level loops its probably best to avoid testing a loops in the syntax diagram (just) once.

[77] Beizer, *Black-Box Testing*, p 77-79
[78] J.C. Huang, *Software Error Detection through Testing and Analysis*, Wily publishing, 2009

## INVALID INPUTS

Finally, syntax testing typically requires not only testing valid inputs, but invalid ones as well. Here the work put into defining the valid syntax via the syntax diagram can be reused for systematically identifying invalid inputs.

Figure 7-2 illustrates three examples of how to "mutate"[79] the valid syntax diagram of Figure 7-1 to produce invalid inputs. Do note, as conventional wisdom in error testing is to try one error test at a time to prevent error masking, these variations would likely be tried one at a time, not all at once. The point of the figure is simply to highlight three common approaches to identifying invalid inputs.

---

[79] See Ammann and Offutt, *Introduction to Software Testing*, for more ideas on mutation testing. Boris Beizer, *Black-Box Testing* refers to this as "dirty syntax" testing.

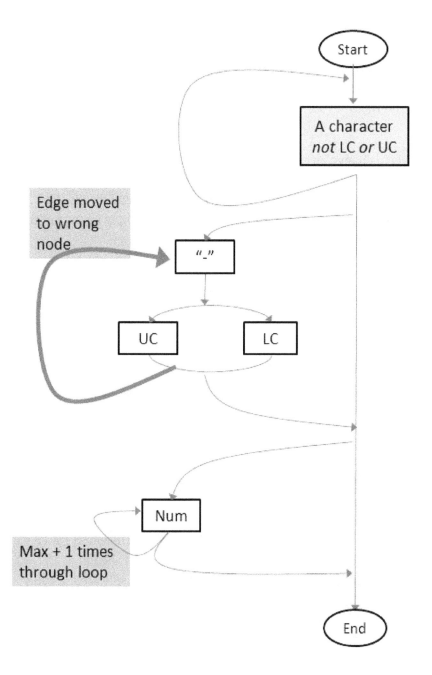

Figure 7-2 Syntax of *invalid* user login ID described as "mutated" version of valid syntax diagram of Figure 7-1

141

Working from top to bottom in the diagram, the first approach illustrated in Figure 7-2 is to modify a *node*, switching it from what is valid, to what is invalid. In this example the node has been changed to indicate trying "A character *not* LC *or* UC". For example, this change (in isolation of the other mutated changes of Figure 7-2) would produce invalid IDs like "#smith-jones", i.e. the ID starts off with an invalid character.

A second approach is to change an *edge* in the diagram. In this case the edge has been moved to terminate in the wrong place, the hyphen node. This change (again, in isolation of the other mutated changes of Figure 7-2) would produce invalid inputs that involved repetition of the hyphen character. For example instead of the valid user login ID "smith-jones", one might have "s-m-i-t-h-j-o-n-e-s".

The third approach is to use the *boundary value* on some loop and exceed the max allowed times through the loop, i.e. generate more characters than are allowed.

As you might expect, one can get really creative with this approach and generate lots and lots of invalid inputs! The judicious use of a little error guessing or focusing on the most common paths through the diagram might help you maximize your bang for the buck with a limited number of invalid input tests.

## REGULAR EXPRESSIONS

Whereas the validation of inputs by an application might have once been seen as a "nice to have" against fat-fingered users, in the era of web-based applications it has moved to the forefront in the fight against cyber-attacks. Organizations such as Open Web Application Security Project (OWASP) promote validating all user supplied inputs as a simple an effective tool for fighting some of the worst cyber-attacks, e.g. SQL injection and other "injection" style attacks. And regular expressions have become key as a tool to allow developers to specify what a valid input is ( called "white-listing" in software security lingo ) and for checking user input at run-time.

For testers, regular expressions are used a bit differently. They are still used to specify the input space of valid inputs (and the tester may even be able to re-use the work the development team may have done in this regard) but rather than then using that description to validate inputs at run-time, the tester uses them to design a finite number of inputs on which to test the application. We are back to partitioning the input space into equivalence classes – valid and invalid -- given some regular expression.

There are a number of good books that discuss regular expressions from the standpoint of test design.[80] Many however have enough of a formal slant to discourage (read "eyes glaze over") would-be testers with a non-computer science or non-programming background. So one goal I have here is to try to provide a 20/80 (the 20% that will probably give you 80% of the bang for the buck) look at regular expressions.

A second goal is to make a bit more specific how regular expressions relate to equivalence partitioning and boundary value analysis. A point that doesn't always come across in discussing the use of regular expressions in test design.

## A 20/80 VIEW OF REGULAR EXPRESSIONS
Regular expressions are just a compact notation to allow you to describe a string of characters, e.g. the input to a use case scenario. Let's start off with some good news; any input's syntax described as a syntax diagram without recursive nodes (like what we covered in the previous section) can be re-cast as a regular expression, and vice versa.[81]

Why is this good news? Because all the test design tricks for directed graphs (syntax diagrams and control flow graphs both being directed graphs; see Chapter 4's Control Flow Graphs: Adjusting the Rigor of Test Design) work with regular expressions.

So from fewest to most paths through a regular expression (and remember, a path is an equivalence class) the tester can ramp up the rigor from node coverage, to edge

---

[80] For those wanting to dive deep, Beizer's Software Testing Techniques, 2nd edition is probably the classic to begin with.
[81] Syntax diagrams allow for non-terminal recursive nodes. The equivalent notation for syntax diagrams is Extended Backus-Naur Form (EBNF), kind of like regular expressions on steroids! For a more technical description, see Ammann & Offutt's *Introduction to Software Testing*. We're going to cover recursion in the next section, Recursive Definitions.

coverage (it will make more sense to call this "decision coverage" for regular expressions; we'll get to that soon), basis path coverage, and all path coverage.

Let's once again return to our **Do Book Search** use case (refer back to Figure 4-1) user login ID example: *"The user ID is a name, using upper or lower case letters, possibly hyphenated to allow for possible hyphenated surnames, with an optional number at the end to distinguish multiple persons with the same name".* In the previous section we used a syntax diagram to describe the syntax. Now let's do the same thing as a regular expression.

Regular expressions provide us with just a few basic notational tools for describing inputs. First, let's say that "LC" stands for any lower-case letter. Then a simple regular expression would be the one letter input:

LC

This describes such IDs as "a", "b", "c" and so on.

But we also said we would allow upper-case as well, so we might say that "UC" stands for any upper-case letter, then we could write a regular expression like this; the vertical bar just means one or the other:

LC | UC

So we've now got a regular expression that describes a one character ID, either upper case or lower case. But we need to be able to have more than a single character for an ID, so next we introduce some notation – the superscript "+" -- that says we repeat a pattern (here inside the parenthesis) one (*at least one*) or more times:

( LC | UC )$^+$

Now we've described such login IDs as "d", "D", "Denney", "denney", "dEnney"; any string of one or more characters, lowercase or uppercase. We now have enough notation to allow us to describe hyphenated names, i.e. a hyphenated ID is just one made of two sets of strings separated by a hyphen "-":

( LC | UC )$^+$, "-", ( LC | UC )$^+$

The commas in this regular expression just say that the strings appears sequentially, one after another. We now have described such IDs as "d-D", "D-d", "Denney", "Smith-Jones".

Do remember however that the use of a hyphenated name as an ID was as option, not mandatory, so we need some notation to let us specify that something is optional; we do that with a set of brackets [...] around the bits that are not mandatory:

( LC | UC )⁺, [ "-", ( LC | UC )⁺]

Finally, we'd like to say that the ID can, if desired, have a number on the very end, to allow multiple people with the same name to use their name and keep them distinct. We denote that with a star superscript "*". It works like the "+" except it says something repeats *zero* or more times, rather than one or more times. And let's say that NUM means any single digit, 0 through 9. Here's our completed description of all possible inputs for the login ID:

( LC | UC )⁺, [ "-", ( LC | UC )⁺], NUM*

This describes such IDs as Denney, Denney013, Smith-Jones, Smith-Jones9, and so on.

So all we needed were these few simple notational tools

| to indicate the occurrence of one thing or another

+ to indicate something repeats one or more times

* to indicate something repeats zero or more times

, to indicate one thing follows after another

[ .. ] to indicate something as being optional

( .. ) to indicate groupings of things

Notice that LC, UC and NUM were just conventions we made up; we could have been more explicit and used our regular expression notation to specify all the valid digits we meant by NUM, but unless we plan on doing test design to that level – e.g. considering that Denney10 vs. Denney11 be separate tests – we don't need to go to that level of detail.

## CYCLOMATIC COMPLEXITY OF A REGULAR EXPRESSION

This is a good time to step back, look at this regular expression, and convince yourself it's describing the same set of possible inputs as the syntax diagrams of Figure 7-1. To help with that Figure 7-3 compares the two side by side.

Two thick horizontal bars divide the syntax diagram into three segments; the gray box in each segment shows the equivalent regular expression for that segment of the syntax diagram.

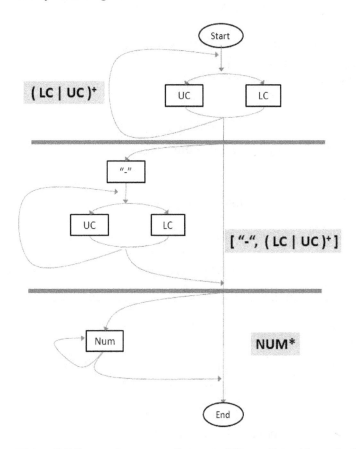

Figure 7-3 Comparing syntax diagram of Figure 7-1 with equivalent regular expression

146

Just as we are able to calculate the cyclomatic complexity from a syntax diagram, we can calculate the cyclomatic complexity from the corresponding regular expression. Let's see how.

Notice in Figure 7-3 that that "|", "+", "*" and "[..]" all correspond to points in the graph where branching takes place: a decision is made to go one way or another. In the same way that we were able to calculate the cyclomatic complexity of the graph by counting regions (which are formed by branching paths) and adding one, we can do the same with a regular expression by counting the number of decision operators in the regular expression and adding one. The one caveat to this being that "*" is counted as two separate decision operators; this makes sense if you consider that NUM* is just short-hand for [NUM+] which is two decisions ("[..]" is counted once as a pair).

Figure 7-4 illustrates the counting of decision operators in our regular expression for the  user login ID. Taking the number of decision operators (seven), plus one, equals 8, the cyclomatic complexity of the regular expression. This lets us know right away we'll need *no more than* 8 tests (one per path; and remember a path is an equivalence class!) for node or edge coverage, exactly eight for basis path coverage, and 8 or more if we deemed it important to shoot for all path coverage (refer back Syntax Diagrams in this chapter, and to Control Flow Graphs in Chapter 4 for a refresher on all this).

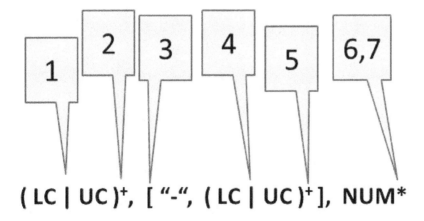

Figure 7-4 Cyclomatic complexity of regular expression: decision operators plus 1

In addition to calculating cyclomatic complexity from a regular expression as a basis for estimating the number of tests needed, we can also quickly identify boundary tests for these looping operators, plus "+" and star "*".

As with directed graphs, boundary value testing relates to the number of times a test executes through these looping operators. Figure 7-5 shows a directed graph with a loop to node N, and the equivalent regular expression $N^+$ We've already discussed boundary values for loops in directed graphs in the context of syntax diagrams. Those same boundary values, and the correspondence between directed graphs and regular expressions, provides the following boundary values for the plus operator "+" in regular expressions:

> zero times through a directed graph loop = $N^1$
>
> one time through a directed graph loop = $N^2$
>
> max times through a directed graph loop = $N^{max+1}$

Directed graph loop.
Boundary values for
times through loop:
0, 1 .. Max

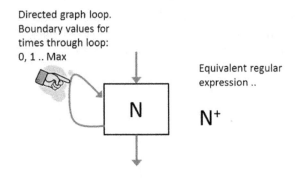

Equivalent regular
expression ..

$N^+$

Figure 7-5 Directed graph loop for some node N and its equivalent regular expression $N^+$

So the boundary values for the plus operator "+" are one, two and some max value.

The boundary values for the star operator "*" are zero, one, two and many. This makes sense if you recall an expression like N* is just short-hand for [N+].

## INVALID INPUTS

As with syntax diagrams, the work done on defining the valid inputs via a regular expression is easily reused for identifying invalid inputs to test. By selectively "mutating" parts of the regular expression, a new expression is derived that describes variants of invalid inputs.

The regular expression below is the equivalent of the syntax diagram for invalid inputs of Figure 7-2 which showed three different approaches to mutation: changing a node from a valid to invalid value; re-directing an edge to the wrong place; exceeding max times through a loop. The same techniques apply here, but are recast into the regular expression:

$$\text{Character\_not\_LC\_or\_UC}^+, \ (\text{"-"}, \ (\text{LC} \mid \text{UC} \ ))^*, \ [ \ \text{NUM} \mid \text{NUM}^{\ max+1 \ times} \ ]$$

It's worth re-iterating; Conventional wisdom in error testing is to try one error test at a time to prevent error masking, so these variations from the valid regular expression would be done one at a time, not all at once.

## REGULAR EXPRESSIONS VS. DIRECTED GRAPHS: WHICH IS BETTER?

One question you might very well be asking yourself at this point is if all regular expressions can be re-cast in syntax diagram form, and vice versa (barring a syntax diagrams with recursion), which is better? And you probably already know the answer is it just depends.

If you are visually oriented you will probably find syntax diagrams easier to use.

On the other hand, as this example shows, regular expressions are much more compact. We've stated in one line what takes a page for a directed graph.

My own personal experience is that often times if I am having a hard time capturing the description of an input with one, switching to the other often does the trick. [82]

---

[82] This seems to be a common theme with equivalent notations. For example, Michael Jackson's *Software Requirements & Specifications: A lexicon of practice, principles and prejudices* asks the same question about JSP trees and finite state machines. His short answer to the question is that "..some strings are much more easily described in one notation than the other".

And, doing both can be a great way to sanity check one with the other. If the cyclomatic complexity of the syntax graph does not match that of the equivalent regular expression, it's a sign one or the other is wrong and needs to be corrected before trying to design tests.

## RECURSIVE DEFINITIONS

The last technique we'll look at for input testing is recursion.

A recursive definition is one which *"first defines one or more base, or starting, cases (or instances) of some concept. It then defines additional instances of the concept by stating how these additional instances can be constructed or obtained from previously defined instances".*[83]

As this definition relates to input testing, the "concept" we'll be defining is the domain of an input. Recursion is one of those topics that people are sometimes intimidated by, in part because it seems counter intuitive to define something in terms of itself. But it is truly a Swiss Army knife for defining, partitioning and doing boundary value analysis of all types of inputs (and outputs) be they numeric in nature, sets of things, Boolean or syntactic.

### *EXAMPLE 1: NUMERIC OUTPUT*
Let's start with an example frequently used to illustrate recursive definitions, calculating the factorial of a number.  While perhaps overly used as an example, it serves a couple of purposes here from a testing perspective, the first of which is to illustrate what has been mentioned several times already: equivalence partitioning and boundary value analysis work for *outputs* as well as inputs. In the case here the input is simple; some non-negative integer. So this is a good example of when it sometimes pays to focus on equivalence partitioning and boundary value analysis of the output instead.

Second, it provides an example where the use case scenario may be quite simple; the point being when doing use case driven testing, you might have a simple scenario

---

[83] Robert Causey, *Logic, Sets and Recursion, 2nd edition,* 2005.

where the crux of the testing problem is the partitioning of the input, or output as the case is here.

Finally, it provides an example of numeric partitioning beyond those typified in the literature, namely those like my previous example of partitioning a numeric range from -200 through +200.

Recall that standard notation for the factorial of a non-negative number, N, is N!, and is defined as the product of N times all integers down to 1. For example, 3! is calculated by 3 x 2 x 1 = 6.

Let's suppose we have some use case scenario that produces as an *output* the factorial of some input. The domain of the input – which we'll denote by N -- is the set of non-negative integers. Rather than use equivalence partitioning and boundary value analysis on the input, we decide to apply it to the output.

We begin by defining the range[84] of the output as a recursive definition. A recursive definition provides one or more "starting points", called base cases – i.e. cases which can't be decomposed further into other descriptions -- followed by one or more recursive rules which describe how all other cases can be obtained from the rules and base cases. [85]

Here's the recursive definition of the factorial of a number, N:

(b1) 0! = 1

(r1) for N >0, N! = N x (N-1)!

I've labeled the base case and recursive rule b1 and r1, respectively, for reasons we'll see in a moment. In words, base case b1 says as a starting point the factorial of zero is one. Recursive rule r1 says to get the factorial of any

---

[84] The term "range" is standard nomenclature for the set of all possible values of the output of a function or binary relation. It's the same concept as the "domain" of an input, but applies to the output instead.
[85] I put "starting points" in quotes because, though defined as such, in practice, with some problems you may find it easier to begin description with the recursive rules.

other number N greater than 0, multiply N times the factorial of N-1. That's the recursive part.

Aside from what may likely be your first question, "Why is the factorial of zero equal to one?!" (which is out of scope for this book, but it does make for interesting reading; Google away!), your next question may be, "And how does this apply to input testing?!"

Well, as we've already discussed, equivalence partitioning and boundary value analysis are important techniques in input testing, and recursive definitions provide a means of applying those techniques. By describing the input or output as a recursive definition we've begun the process of identifying equivalence classes. We reduce an infinite set of inputs (or outputs) into a small number of rules, the combinations of which describe all inputs, and the combinations of which can be tested with tools we've already seen: control flow graphs and regular expressions.

Every calculation of factorial is covered by some sequence of applying these two rules. Examples of paths through rules r1 and b1 and how they relate to factorial are shown in Figure 7-6. Just as paths through a syntax diagram can be viewed as equivalence classes, so too are paths through the various sequences of recursive rules (refer back to Syntax Diagrams in this chapter for a refresher on how directed graphs relate to equivalence classes).

    path b1 describes 0!
    path r1, b1 describes 1!
    path r1, r1, b1 describes 2!
    path r1, r1, r1, b1 describes 3!
    path r1, r1, r1, r1, b1 describes 4!
    Etc..

Figure 7-6 Example paths through rules r1 and b1

We can describe all possible paths through rules r1 and b1 with the control flow / call graph of Figure 7-7. In the graph rules b1 and r1 appear as nodes. Every factorial can be described by moving through the nodes of the graph from the start to the end. The solid arrows (edges of the graph) from the start node show which of the rules can be applied first, in this case either r1 or b1. The solid arrow from rule b1 to the end illustrates that all recursion will end with that base case. The dotted arrows in the graph show recursive calls from rule r1 to itself, and to the base case b1.

Seeing the recursive definition of factorial put into the format of a control flow / call graph is helpful in understanding that the techniques we used for control flow graphs work here with recursive definitions, for example estimating needed tests by calculating the cyclomatic complexity; and test design via node, edge and basis path coverage (refer back to Control Flow Graphs:  Adjusting the Rigor of Test Design).[86]

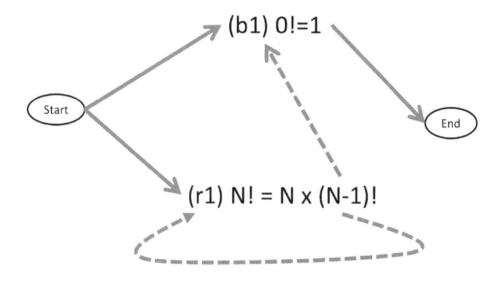

Figure 7-7 Control flow / call graph for recursive definition of factorial

----

[86] We could have also described all possible paths through rules r1 and b1 as this regular expression. You may sometimes find the more compact notation helpful: r1* b1

## Node, Edge, Basis Path Coverage for Factorial

Let's conclude with a look at how to design tests for factorial based on node, edge and basis path coverage. First, we can quickly calculate the cyclomatic complexity of the control flow / call graph for factorial: 2 regions plus 1 = 3. So 3 tests is an upper bound for edge (and hence node) coverage, and an exact number for basis path coverage.

Node coverage we can achieve in as few as a single test:

calculating 1! covers path start, r1, b1, end

Edge coverage we can achieve with as few as two tests:

calculating 0! covers path start, b1, end
calculating 2! covers path start, r1, r1, b1, end

Basis path coverage we can achieve in three tests:

calculating 0! covers path start, b1, end
calculating 1! covers path start, r1, b1, end
calculating 2! covers path start, r1, r1, b1, end

Finally, a boundary value test can be achieved by making sure we go through the recursive call of r1 to itself a maximum number of times. Let's say, just as an example, that the user interface on which the factorial will be displayed limits the output to four integers. So 7!, which equals 5040, is the largest number we can compute:

calculating 7! covers path start, r1, r1, r1, r1, r1, r1, r1, b1, end

Factorial is an example of *linear* recursion where a recursive rule makes just *one* recursive call. In the next example we'll look at recursive rules that make two recursive calls. This is called *binary* recursion. In general, you can have any number of recursive calls in a recursive rule, i.e. N-ary recursion. The key point to remember is that regardless – linear, binary, n-ary -- paths through the various sequences of base and recursive rules is a way to define equivalence classes for an input or output.

*EXAMPLE 2: SYNTAX TESTING FOR DO BOOK SEARCH USE CASE*

Recall back in Chapter 4 we wrote an initial test case for the "happy path" scenario, of the **Do Book Search** use case of our library book management system (see Figure 4-4). One of the steps in that test case was to perform a book search based on title:

- Test step: User types keywords from the title of a book of interest.
- Expected result: System finds all books with titles that contain the keywords, and displays them in list form.

The input to this test step is a book title keyword search. As the test stands, it would be up to the tester at this point to be creative in deciding the queries to try.

For our final example of recursive definitions, we'll specify the syntax of that query, then derive test inputs we can use with the test case of Figure 4-4.

## Tool Support: Prolog

If we are going to design tests from the recursive definition of an input, it would be good to have some confidence that the definition we write actually says what we think it says! For simple inputs we can usually inspect the recursive definition we write (or one provided by a developer) and mentally persuade ourselves it's correct.

For non-trivial recursive definitions of an input (like the one at hand) this can be a lot tougher. As discussed earlier, while in theory you don't need tool support for things like pairwise testing, tools such as James Bach's Allpairs certainly make the going easier (refer back to Chapter 5). The same applies with test design from non-trivial recursive definitions of inputs. For complicated recursive definitions it is nice to have tool support to:

- Help determine if the definition we write actually says what we *think* it says
- Help us write tests by acting a bit like a "code coverage" tool, but for rules

One way to address this problem is to build a runnable specification using some programming language; for this example we'll be using Prolog.

Prolog (Programming in logic) originated in the early 70s as a popular tool for artificial intelligence, problem solving, game playing, symbolic computing, natural language understanding (defining syntax) and expert systems[87].  And the formal methods testing community recognized its potential as a tool to aid in test case generation [88], [89],[90]

To quote Clocksin and Mellish[91] "Prolog is a conversational language, which means that you and the computer carry out a kind of conversation." As it relates to our problem the conversation goes like this.

We define the syntax of the input to the **Do Book Search** use case and load it into Prolog.  Figure 7-8 shows the Prolog rules for the syntax for the book keyword search. Then Prolog prompts you with "| ?-", kind of like asking *"OK, What is your question?".*  What you then ask is *"Here's an example of a book query. Can you confirm that this example is valid by the recursive definition I loaded?".*

Prolog will then respond "yes" if your example is a valid input according to the definition. Prolog will respond "no" or issue some failure message if the example you provided doesn't match with the definition you provided; your mental model of what you think is a valid example doesn't jive with what you defined as a valid syntax. One or both is wrong.

Additionally, given a keyword search, we can have Prolog show us the recursive rules that were covered by the query.

---

[87] Richard Denney and Scott Guthery, Reconfiguration advisor, United States Patent 4815076
[88] S. Gerhart, "A test data generation method using Prolog," Wang Inst. of Grad. Studies, Tech. Rep. TR85-02, 1985.
[89] L Bougé et.al., "Application of PROLOG to test sets generation from algebraic specifications", *Proceedings of the International Joint Conference on Theory and Practice of Software Development (TAPSOFT) on Formal Methods and Software, Vol.2: Colloquium on Software Engineering (CSE)*, 1985
[90] Richard Denney, "Test-Case Generation from Prolog-Based Specifications", *IEEE Software, special issue on testing*, Volume 8 Issue 2, March 1991
[91] Clocksin and Mellish, Programming in Prolog, 2nd edition, 1984.

```
/* BASE CASE */

search X :- atom(X), rule base.

/* RECURSIVE RULES */

search (X, More):- rule r1, search X, search More.
search X or Y :- rule r2, search X, search Y.
search not X :- rule r3, search X.
```

Figure 7-8 Prolog rules defining syntax of book keyword search

## Review of Recursive Definition

Let's walk through the rules of Figure 7-8 and discuss how to read them. The goal here is not to teach Prolog, just understand enough to see the recursion that is taking place. These two lines are just comments and appear above the one base case and three recursive rules, respectively.

```
/* BASE CASE*/
/* RECURSIVE RULES */
```

Rules in Prolog consist of a head and body, separated by the symbol ":-" which can be read like "if", or "where", or "given". You can think of it like a function or procedure: the head shows the procedure argument list, the body shows what the procedure executes. So the head of rule r2, the second recursive rule, takes two arguments, X and Y. Here's the head:

```
search X or Y
```

The body of rule r2 is

```
rule r2, search X, search Y
```

Putting it all together the rule reads "search X or Y" is a valid search query if "search X" and "search Y" are themselves valid search queries. That's the recursion.

Each rule is labeled with one of these terms: rule base, rule r1, rule r2 and rule r3. These are for reference only as we talk about the definition; they don't have anything to do with the search query syntax per se. They do serve one other purpose, as trace statements letting the test designer (and you the reader) see the sequence of rules that are being used in a query. More on this shortly.

### Base Case

The first rule, the base case, says that any simple atomic term is a keyword search in its own right. In the following example, we ask Prolog if "titanic" is a valid query (we're interested in books on the Titanic). The line following our query is Prolog's response, "yes", it is a valid book search query, and our trace statement shows us the path through the rules that were used, in this case, just the base case.

> | ?- search titanic.
> base yes

### Recursive Rule R1

Now to the recursive rules. Recursive rule r1 says that any string of terms in parentheses, separated by commas (and as with Google search, let's assume a comma is treated as "and") is a valid search query if the first term of the query X is itself a valid search, and the rest ( More ) is a valid search. This is the recursive part, it's what is called binary recursion, i.e. this rule makes two recursive calls.

> | ?- search (gone, with, the, wind).
> r1 base r1 base r1 base base yes

In this example we see that a combination of rules r1 used recursively on itself (both of the two recursive calls resolve to rule r1) and the base are used.

### Recursive Rule R2

Recursive rule r2 of Figure 7-8 says that any query like "search X or Y" is valid if X and Y are both valid search queries themselves. Again, a rule using binary recursion.

> | ?- search (gone or went, with, the, wind or breeze).

r1 r2 base base r1 base r1 base r2 base base yes

In this example we see that we have now exercised rules r1, r2 and the base.

*Recursive Rule R3*

Turning to our last recursive rule, rule r3 says that "not X" is a valid query if X itself is a valid search query. That's the recursive part. We might for example be interested in searching for books on jobs (employment), but don't want "steve" (Steve Jobs) in the title.

> | ?- search (finding, jobs, not steve).
> r1 base r1 base r3 base yes

This example has exercised rule r1, recursively calling itself, plus rule r3, and the base.

From the examples above are you seeing how Prolog used as an aid in test design acts a bit like a code coverage tool in unit testing? A developer doing unit testing often devises tests from a black-box standpoint, runs them on his or her code, and uses a code coverage tool to determine which segments of code, and paths through the code, were, and weren't covered. Additional tests are then devised to cover the gaps of the latter. It's the same idea here, but rather than code coverage, we are doing rule coverage. We devise a set of tests – keyword searches – run them through Prolog and see what rules, and combinations of rules, were covered. We then design additional tests to increase coverage.

## Test Design

We now turn to test design from the rules of Figure 7-8. To kick things off we first build a control flow graph similar to that from our previous factorial example (refer back to Figure 7-7). The control flow graph for the Prolog recursive rules is shown in Figure 7-9.

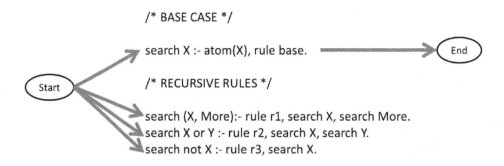

/* BASE CASE */

search X :- atom(X), rule base.

/* RECURSIVE RULES */

search (X, More):- rule r1, search X, search More.
search X or Y :- rule r2, search X, search Y.
search not X :- rule r3, search X.

Start

End

Figure 7-9 Control flow graph for book keyword search

One difference you will note between the control flow / call graph for the factorial example of Figure 7-7, and the control flow graph of Figure 7-9, the former included the recursive calls between rules. The factorial example was simple enough to allow them to be shown. The call graph for the rules of Figure 7-9 is too complex to display on a single graph so we'll be tackling the call coverage rule by rule.

We'll proceed as before by first designing tests for node coverage, then proceed to edge coverage. The problem is complicated enough we won't try for basis path coverage, but the same process demonstrated for factorial would be used if we chose to do so.

### Node Coverage (Rule Coverage)
The simplest, minimal form of coverage for a recursive definition is simply to design enough tests to ensure each rule has been used at least once. And because rules are nodes of the graph of Figure 7-9, this is equivalent to node coverage.

For the recursive definition of Figure 7-9 we can cover all rules with as few as a single test. The Prolog trace statements (second line) show that indeed all rules – recursive and base -- were used in this query:

> | ?- search (gone or left, with, the, wind or breeze, not hurricane or tornado).
> r1 r2 base base r1 base r1 base r1 r2 base base r2 r3 base base yes

While we can certainly cover all rules with as few as a single test, you'll agree no doubt, this is probably the bare minimum input testing we'd want. Still, in the world of budgeting time in test design, this is an option for saving time on a seldom used,

160

less critical use case's input in order to spend more time on the input of a critical use case.

## Edge Coverage, Part I (Start Node Edges)

To reiterate, the control flow graph of Figure 7-9 is like the control / call graph for factorial we saw back in Figure 7-7 except that recursive calls between rules are not shown; there are too many to cleanly display on a single graph. In this and the next section we'll break test design for edge coverage of Figure 7-9 in two parts: we'll first cover the edges shown, then we'll go rule by rule to cover the recursive calls showing the edges being covered as we proceed.

Looking at the control flow graph of Figure 7-9 all queries the user can pose in searching for a book are described by moving from start to end, with the three recursive rules making recursive calls to one another "in the middle". Recursive rules reach the end by a final recursive call to the base case which in turn leads to the end node. While our previous example of node coverage used all the rules, it only covered one edge in the control flow graph of Figure 7-9. This is illustrated with highlighting in Figure 7-10. In other words, the query we used for node coverage was based on rule r1 at the very top level of recursion, it in turn calling all other rules.

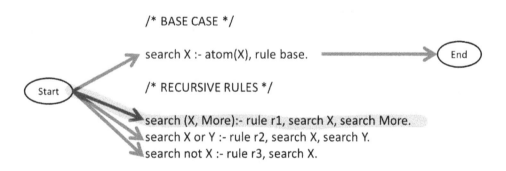

Figure 7-10 Previous example of node coverage only covered one edge of control flow graph

Our first step in edge coverage is to make sure we have enough test queries to cover the four edges radiating from the start node of the control flow graph of Figure 7-9. By visual inspection of the graph, we can tell we'll need a minimum of four, i.e. one for each of the four edges. Here's four that do the trick; notice from the trace

161

statements below each query that each query leads off with a different one of the base case and recursive rules at the top-most level of recursion.

> | ?- search scarlett.
> base yes

> | ?- search (gone, with, wind).
> r1 base r1 base base yes

> | ?- search (scarlett, ohara) or (gone, with, the, wind).
> r2 r1 base base r1 base r1 base r1 base base yes

> | ?- search not (hurricane, tornado, cyclone).
> r3 r1 base r1 base base yes

## *Edge Coverage, Part II (Recursive Call Coverage)*

As mentioned several times, but worth emphasizing once more, the control flow graph of Figure 7-9 is like the control / call graph for factorial we saw back in Figure 7-7. But for Figure 7-9 there are too many recursive calls to cleanly display on the graph.

The final step in edge coverage of Figure 7-9 is to use the same technique used in structural or white-box testing to do *call coverage* of a call graph. [92] We're just applying it to calls between recursive rules rather than between, say subroutines or methods, of a program.

We'll proceed in test design by visiting each of the recursive rules – r1, r2, r3 -- writing call coverage tests for each.

### Call Coverage, rule r1

Figure 7-11 and Figure 7-12 show our recursive definition, broken into two figures to make it easier to see. Figure 7-11 shows calls (think paths over edges in the graph) from the *first* recursive call to the heads of all other possible rules it can resolve to. Figure 7-12 shows calls from the *second* recursive call to the heads of all other possible rules it can resolve to.

---

[92] Ammann and Offutt, Introduction to Software Testing, pp 65

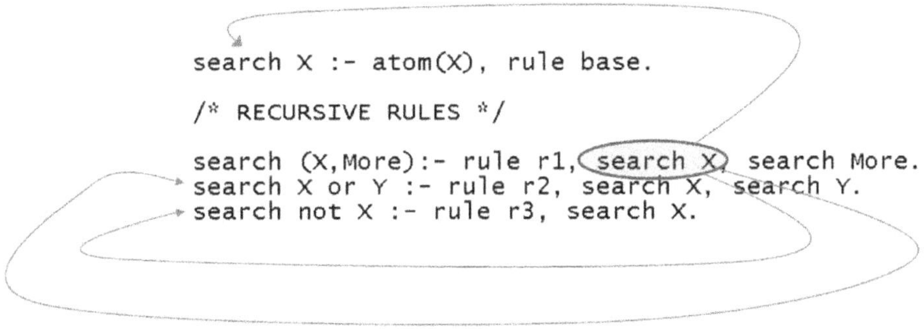

```
search X :- atom(X), rule base.

/* RECURSIVE RULES */

search (X,More):- rule r1, search X  search More.
search X or Y :- rule r2, search X, search Y.
search not X :- rule r3, search X.
```

Figure 7-11 Recursive calls for rule r1, call 1

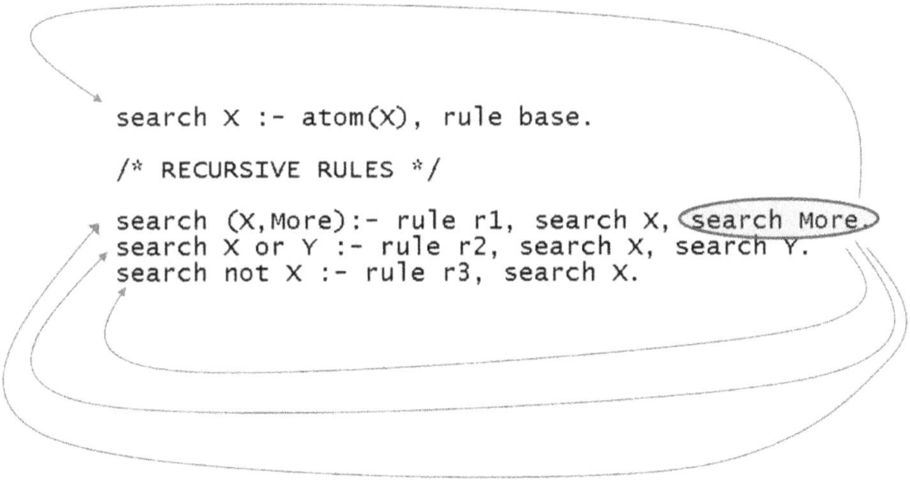

```
search X :- atom(X), rule base.

/* RECURSIVE RULES */

search (X,More):- rule r1, search X, search More
search X or Y :- rule r2, search X, search Y.
search not X :- rule r3, search X.
```

Figure 7-12 Recursive calls for rule r1, call 2

What we'll do now is systematically identify book search queries that cover all the calls (edges in graph from the call to a resolving rule) of rule r1. Let's start with this example, a search for a particular book, Cormac McCarthy's *All the Pretty Horses*.

    | ?- search (pretty, horses).
    r1 base base yes

Looking at the trace statements, the resultant rule path executed by the first and second recursive calls are shown. Highlighting has been used to better see the rule paths associated with the two separate calls. What we see from the trace statements is that the path from call1 to the base case has been covered (the first highlight), as well as the path from call2 to the base case (second highlight).

Now we try another query.

> | ?- search (all, pretty, horses).
> r1 base r1 base base yes

As the trace statement shows, we have now covered the path from call 1 to the base case (first highlight; a repeat of coverage from the previous query), and the path from call 2 to rule r1 (second highlight).

Next query.

> | ?- search (all or some, pretty or horses).
> r1 r2 base base r2 base base yes

We have now covered the path from call1 to rule r2, and from call2 to rule r2.

Another query.

> | ?- search (not steve, finding, jobs, not apple).
> r1 r3 base r1 base r1 base r3 base yes

We have now covered the path from call1 to rule r3 (first highlight), and from call2 to rule r3 (second highlight; this is occurring at a lower level of recursion)

We've now achieved 100% call coverage for rule r1. Let's summarize.

In Figure 7-11 we have covered all paths from call1 to the base case, rule r2, and rule r3.[93] In Figure 7-12 we have covered all paths from call2 to the base case, rule r1, rule r2 and rule r3.

---

[93] Note there is no recursive call path from rule r1, call1, back to itself, rule r1.

## Call Coverage, rule r2

As before with call1, we now systematically identify book search queries that cover the paths from rule r2's two calls (this is again binary recursion) to the rules to which they can resolve. In this case, both call1 and call2 can resolve to the same rules. The paths for both rules are jointly shown in Figure 7-13, just be aware there are actually two sets of edges.

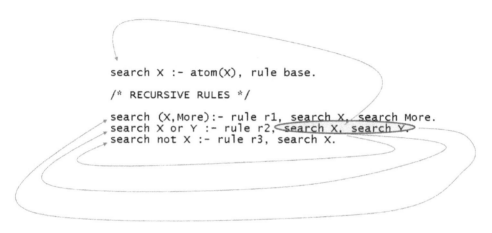

```
search X :- atom(X), rule base.

/* RECURSIVE RULES */

search (X,More):- rule r1, search X, search More.
search X or Y :- rule r2, search X, search Y
search not X :- rule r3, search X.
```

Figure 7-13 Recursive calls for rule r2, both calls

Below are four queries that achieve call coverage for both calls of rule r2. In each case, the paths covered by each call are shown highlighted.

| ?- search (titanic or bismarck).
r2 base base yes

| ?- search (all, pretty, horses) or (gone, with, wind).
r2 r1 base r1 base base  r1 base r1 base base yes

| ?- search (lonesome or dove) or (comanche or moon).
r2 r2 base base r2 base base yes

| ?- search not lonesome or not doves.
r2 r3 base r3 base yes

We've now achieved 100% call coverage for rule r2.

165

## Call Coverage, rule r3

This brings us to our last rule, rule r3, for which we need tests for call coverage. This rule is linear recursive, it has only one recursive call. The paths from the call to the heads of all rules the call resolves to are shown in Figure 7-14.

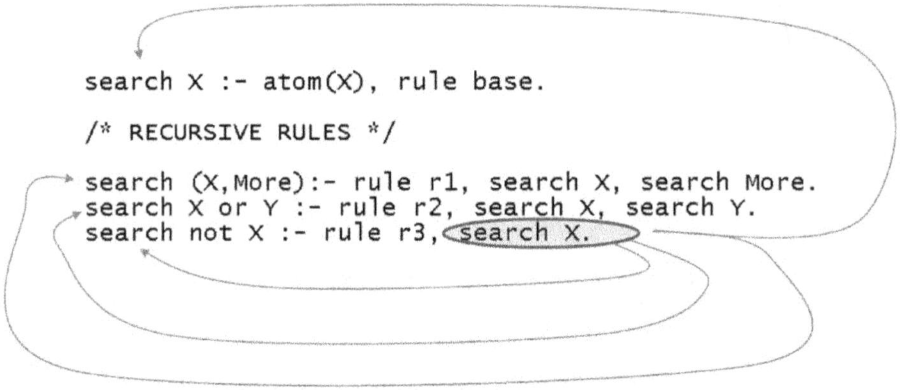

```
search X :- atom(X), rule base.

/* RECURSIVE RULES */

search (X,More):- rule r1, search X, search More.
search X or Y :- rule r2, search X, search Y.
search not X :- rule r3, search X.
```

Figure 7-14 Recursive calls for rule r3

The following four queries cover all paths in Figure 7-14.

> | ?- search not titanic.
> r3 base yes
>
> | ?- search not (apache, gold, yaqui, silver).
> r3 r1 base r1 base r1 base base yes
>
> | ?- search not (comanche or moon).
> r3 r2 base base yes
>
> | ?- search not not titanic.
> r3 r3 base yes

With this we have now achieved 100% call coverage for rules r1, r2 and r3.

### Closing Thoughts on Recursive Definitions

That completes design of the test inputs for the book title keyword search, part of the "happy path" scenario of the **Do Book Search** use case. These test inputs would be used in conjunction with the test we initially started back in Chapter 4 (see Figure 4-4). That test would be run for each of the test inputs we have identified in this example.

Boundary value testing with recursion is just a matter of pushing the nested levels of recursion to the limits of what is allowed in the requirements or by other constraints, e.g. screen real estate or code implementation. Here's an example:

```
| ?- search not not not not not not not not not titanic.
r3 r3 r3 r3 r3 r3 r3 r3 r3 base yes
```

It's worth noting that while some of these examples don't make a lot sense from a content standpoint (e.g. *search not lonesome or not doves*), the goal here is syntax testing, not testing queries that make sense! If the syntax is allowed, it needs to be tested. If it's not, the system needs to restrict it (which again needs to be tested).

Finally, as I think this example has illustrated, the call graph of a recursive definition can get pretty complicated. As with any control flow graph, if we achieve edge coverage we will have also achieved node coverage.  If we achieve basis path coverage (which we didn't illustrate for this example) we will have also achieved edge coverage. In the spirit of always looking for ways to budget time in test design, one can also adapt a "mix and match" strategy. Say, rather than going for 100% edge coverage, we might decide to apply it to one key rule, augmented with say simpler node coverage for the remaining rules.

# CHAPTER REVIEW

Let's review what we've covered in this chapter.

Three techniques were presented for describing inputs as a basis for equivalence partitioning and boundary value testing: syntax diagrams, regular expressions and recursive definitions.

Syntax diagrams, like control flow graphs, are directed graphs. Nodes of the graph represent a character or token. Paths through the graph show the allowed sequence of characters or tokens that make up an input. As a directed graph, we can reuse all the techniques from Chapter 4, Control Flow Graphs: Adjusting the Rigor of Test Design, to decide how much rigor we want to partition the input space into: node coverage, edge coverage, basis path coverage, or even all paths coverage.

Regular expressions are non-graphic (non-visual) cousins of syntax diagrams. Any input's syntax described as a syntax diagram without recursion can be re-cast as a regular expression, and vice versa. This is good news because just as we are able to calculate the cyclomatic complexity from a syntax diagram (to estimate number of needed tests) we can calculate the cyclomatic complexity from the corresponding regular expression. Concepts of varying degrees of rigor apply as well: node coverage, edge coverage, etc.

As a rule of thumb you'll find some problems seem easier to model with regular expressions than with a syntax diagram (and vice versa), hence the usefulness of both.

We concluded with a look at recursive definitions. A recursive definition defines an input (or output) as one or more base cases and recursive rules. For test design we looked at how the rules of recursive definition are modeled with a control flow / call graph, and illustrated node, edge and basis path coverage of such a graph. Because nodes of the graph are the rules of the definition, 100% node coverage assures all rules of the definition have been used. Because recursive calls between rules appear as edges in the graph, 100% edge coverage assures all recursive calls have been covered.

# PART IV: OPERATIONS

## TEST DESIGN AT THE GROUND LEVEL

Starting from Part I of the book, the view of use cases from 30,000 feet, we looked at test design from a collection of use cases that form a use case diagram. In Part II, the view of use cases from 20,000 feet, we looked at test design based on the paths, or scenarios, that collectively form a use case. In Part III, the view of use cases from 10,000 feet, we then focused on test design from a single path of a use case. In this, the final part of the book, we arrive at "ground level": test design from the individual operations, or steps, of a use case scenario.

A use case describes the behavior of an application or system as a sequence of steps -- or "messages"[94] -- some of which result in the invocation of an operation in the system. The operation is the finest level of granularity for which we'll be looking at test design.[95]

For component-based / service oriented architectures, the operations may well correspond to public interfaces common to many use cases in your system, in which case the tests designed for the operation in one use case serves double duty for other use cases.

In Chapter 8 Preconditions, Postconditions and Invariants: Thinking About How Operations Fail, we are going to look at a time tested technique for specifying the expected behavior of abstract data types and objects – *model-based specification* – and apply it to *use case failure analysis*: the analysis of potential ways a use case operation might fail.

In doing so, the reader will learn some things about preconditions and postconditions they forgot to mention in "Use Case 101"! This approach – thinking

---

[94] Rumbaugh, Jacobson and Booch, The UML Reference Manual, 2nd edition, 2004
[95] In UML, operations are implemented as methods on a class, which would be amenable to further decomposition using white-box testing techniques. But from the black-box standpoint we'll stop with the operation.

about failure -- is a powerful risk-driven strategy, focusing testing on detection of high impact defects first while providing development the requirements they need to design systems that fail in a safe way.

Having gained some insight into the true relationship between preconditions, postconditions and invariants via model-based specification, Chapter 9 provides lower-tech ways to identify preconditions that could lead to the failure of an operation.

# Chapter 8 Preconditions, Postconditions and Invariants: Thinking About How Operations Fail

From a black-box testing perspective, preconditions and postconditions are the quintessential tool for describing an use case operation, saying what it does, without saying how. They are ideal for black-box testing, and from a failure analysis standpoint, preconditions play the role of specifying those conditions under which a use case operation is intended to work correctly, and conversely the conditions under which it might fail. A system can then be implemented using techniques such as *design by contract* or *defensive programming*, where methods or routines check their preconditions -- called assertions: they assert what the routine assumes to be true -- before running. If the precondition is false, the routine can handle the exception in a safe fashion, i.e. *fail safe*.[96]

In reality, however, few use cases are produced with preconditions and postconditions of substance enough to test from. If you look at your favorite book on use cases you are likely to find use cases with preconditions, but no postconditions (the significance of which will make sense later), and postconditions with no preconditions. And even when both are present you would likely be hard pressed to tell *what a use case did based solely on the pre and postconditions*. While developers may be willing to keep use cases informal[97] when it comes to failure analysis and test design, something a bit more concrete is needed, hence a number of proposals for making use cases more test-ready have appeared.[98]

In this chapter we look briefly at the history of preconditions and postconditions, and learn what they forgot to tell you in "Use Case 101": *preconditions can be calculated from postconditions*, and often with little more than simple algebra! The usefulness of this fact should be obvious from a black-box testing and failure

---

[96] Neil Storey's *Safety-Critical Computer Systems* discusses the role of *assertions* in safety-critical systems, and Binder, *Testing Object-Oriented Systems* looks at their use in automated testing.

[97] See Alistair Cockburn, "Use Cases, Ten Years Later" for a discussion of this topic.

[98] See for example Binder's Extended Use Cases and David Gelperin's Precise Use Cases.

analysis standpoint: given a black-box's outputs (the postcondition), you can calculate the set of inputs and starting states which produce it (the precondition), and conversely the inputs and starting states which are excluded, could spell system failure, and hence may warrant error handling tests. In this chapter we also discuss invariants, which are to use cases what safety requirements are to safety-critical systems.

## SANITY CHECK BEFORE PROCEEDING

In this chapter you will be looking at preconditions and postconditions of *individual operations* of a use case. This is a different perspective from some use case literature that talks about pre and postconditions of the use case "as a whole".

One consequence of the latter perspective is that the use case community has focused primarily on preconditions that must be satisfied before the use case can *start*. But from a failure analysis and test design standpoint this is not sufficient: there are usually operations (say later in the use case) whose preconditions are to be satisfied by the postcondition of another operation earlier in the same use case; while such preconditions do not prevent the use case from *starting*, their violation can translate into system failure nevertheless.

Another difference to be aware of is that of scope. In some use case literature you will read that preconditions and postconditions should apply to all scenarios of a use case, i.e. to all possible paths through a use case. From a failure analysis and test design standpoint this will usually *not* be true.

In this chapter we'll be dealing with preconditions and postconditions as tied to operations performed by the steps of the use case, and since the steps of a use case vary from scenario to scenario, we should expect that their preconditions and postconditions will vary as well.

To see why this is important, consider: If the postconditions of a use case are – by definition -- so general as to be valid for all possible use case scenarios, they are likely not to be useful as a basis for specifying expected behavior in test design or failure analysis. For example the outputs and final state of a failed attempt to withdraw cash from an ATM are not the same as a successful withdrawal: if your postconditions reflect this, they too will differ; if your postconditions *don't* reflect this, you can't use them to specify the expected behavior of tests.

While the discussion here of preconditions and postconditions of operations is consistent with UML (The UML Reference Manual defines preconditions and postconditions in terms of operations[99]) the chapter could be a little confusing if you read it with the mindset that the only type of use case precondition is one that must be satisfied before the use case starts.

## A Brief History Of Preconditions And Postconditions

Preconditions and postconditions were a relatively recent addition to what Alistair Cockburn, in his article *Use Cases, Ten Years Later,* calls the fully dressed use case. They weren't a part of Jacobson's original use cases, or OMT's scenarios. But though a newcomer to use cases, the history of pre and postconditions goes back to at least the late 1960s with the work of researches like Floyd, Hoare and Dijkstra.[100]

Preconditions and postconditions played a key role in reasoning about programs (Does this program meet its specification?) and later with formal specification languages like VDM (Vienna Development Method) and Z (pronounced "Zed") as a way to specify the behavior of Abstract Data Types. Much of what we today ascribe to being "object-oriented" is rooted in the concept of Abstract Data Types (ADT). This is particularly true of the matter of specifying the *expected behavior* of an object, which is of course an issue of *great* interest to testing. In 1971 David Parnas' introduced "Information Hiding" which wrapped each "design decision" in a module with a defined interface *eliminating the need for details of how the module was programmed.* But of course if you are going to hide the details of the implementation of your new widget from your fellow programmers, you need some way of communicating to them what the widget *does.* By the mid to late 70s two approaches to tackling the problem were underway: the algebraic specification

---

[99] See Rumbaugh et.al., The Unified Modeling Language Reference Manual, Second Edition.
[100] A paper by Cliff Jones, "The Early Search for Tractable Ways of Reasoning about Programs", even traces roots going back to work by pioneers such as Von Neuman and Turing in the late 1940s.

approach, and the model-based specification approach. VDM and Z[101] were outgrowths of the work on the latter. These formal specification languages and techniques in turn influenced the Object-Oriented community, e.g. Bertrand Meyer's Eiffel[102] with its Design by Contract, pre-UML "unified" Object-Oriented methodologies like Fusion[103], and more recently UML's Object Constraint Language (OCL)[104].

Fast forwarding to today, though preconditions and postconditions are now a part of the fully dressed use case, a key facet in their history, one central to their use in reasoning about programs and specifications, has been overlooked a tad. *Preconditions can be calculated from postconditions.* In fact, that was pretty much the point originally; You can calculate preconditions from postconditions – as opposed to intuitively making them up.

This technique is usually described in terms of *Hoare triples*, or *predicate transformer* for calculating the *weakest precondition*, i.e. a technique that transforms one predicate, the postcondition, into another, the precondition. The version of the technique we'll see in this book is basically that used by Z, and in that literature is often just called "calculating the precondition".

Now the intent here is not to say that calculating the precondition is the *only*, or even the *right* way you get preconditions for use cases; even in writing specifications in formal languages like Z, one usually comes up with preconditions in an intuitive sort of way (in the next chapter we'll be looking at additional techniques for spotting preconditions on operations).

But that connection between precondition and postcondition is always there to leverage, e.g. as a way to demonstrate the validity of an intuitively derived precondition, or to tell if there are additional preconditions that have been overlooked. And it turns out to be a handy tool for failure analysis of use cases.

---

[101] For an overview of algebraic and model-based specification see Ian Sommerville, *Software Engineering.*
[102] Bertrand Meyer, *Object-Oriented Software Construction*
[103] Coleman et.al., *Object-Oriented Development: The Fusion Method*
[104] Warmer and Kleppe, *Object Constraint Language: Precise Modeling with UML*

## CALCULATING PRECONDITIONS FROM POSTCONDITIONS

The best way to illustrate this technique is through examples, so let's dive in and work through an example, then step back and evaluate the process.

### USE CASE OVERVIEW

A new on-line merchant has just introduced gift cards. You can buy a gift card online, and have it mailed to a friend. Each card has a unique ID; to buy something you go to the website, log-in using the ID, then buy something. If you have change coming, a check for the difference is mailed to you; this is seen as marketing differentiation from competitors that force the customer to spend the full gift card price or more, or lose the difference.

Figure 8-1 shows the main scenario for the Buy Something With Gift Card use case.

Use Case: **Buy Something With Gift Card**

> Make on-line purchase with gift card receiving change back via check on difference between card value and item purchased.

Main scenario

- Customer goes to web site and logs in with gift card ID
- Customer selects item of interest
- Customer enters address, confirms, and checks-out
- System signals inventory to mail item to address
- System signals accounts payable to mail check for difference between gift card value and price of item

Figure 8-1 Buy Something With Gift Card use case, main scenario

With typical use case description in hand, we are ready to think about how the system, as described by this use case, could fail, and identify preconditions that would guard against such failure.

175

*STEP 1. FIND A "RISKY" POSTCONDITION: MODEL AS AN EQUATION*

First, we identify an operation or step of the use case the postcondition for which we wish to calculate the precondition. In general, it's not safe to assume the postconditions provided (if any) are the only postconditions. You'll need to read the body of the use case and look for operations where outputs are produced, or state is changed, paying particular attention to ones doing "risky things". Looking at our example, this operation certainly fits the bill, so we'll focus on it:

> "System signals accounts payable to mail check for difference between gift card value and price of item"

Next we write the operation's postcondition in the form of a simple equation:

> CheckAmount = GiftCardValue - PriceOfItem

That was pretty easy. It's important to note that the "=" is *not assignment*; it is *equality*, and the equation describes a relationship between the three variables. Use of equality is what allows us to leverage the power of algebra that makes this technique work.[105]

*STEP 2. IDENTIFY A POTENTIAL FAILURE: STATE AN INVARIANT*

This next step is at the heart of this technique so a bit of discussion is in order. In a use case, postconditions are where the action is at. They describe the output produced and state changed by the use case. And it is precisely when you are generating outputs and changing state that the opportunity for really "screwing things up" occurs; as the old saying goes: "To err is human. To really screw up you need a computer". So how does one judge if the computation described by a postcondition is valid, i.e. isn't going to screw something up? To do so we need some statement of what a valid output, or valid system state is. These statements of validity are typically called *invariants*. In the formal methods community they are

---

[105] David Gries and Fred Schneider's, *A Logical Approach to Discrete Math*, provides in depth coverage of equality, equational logic, and leveraging simple algebra style thinking applied to reasoning about programs.

variously called data invariants or state invariants: statements that should always be true about the data and system state being described. In the object-oriented community they are called class invariants: something that should always be true about a class and any object instantiated from it (class invariants were inherited – no pun intended – from the formal methods community, so are quite similar). In the study of program algorithms there are loop invariants: something that should always be true about the loop being programmed (loop as in "While X do Y"). The word "invariant" simply means something that does not vary; is always true. The common denominator in all these invariants is that they set constraints that postconditions should not "violate".

So as a way to sanity check the postconditions of our use case, we introduce the use of invariants. Given these invariants, we can then ask if the computation described by the postcondition preserves them. As it turns out, the answer is usually something like, "Yes, assuming that such and such is true when the computation happens". *And that, is a precondition: the "such and such" that must be true in order that the postcondition preserves the invariant, i.e. nothing gets "screwed up".*

Explanation aside, let's look at the next step. Looking at our postcondition, we ask what bad things could happen with respect to the computation the postcondition is describing? One that comes immediately to mind is cutting a check for more than the gift card was worth; that is literally a money losing proposition. So an invariant for this postcondition – remember something we always want to be true – is that the refund check amount should *never* be more than the value of the gift card:

### Invariant: CheckAmount < GiftCardValue

In the field of safety-critical systems – systems where failures pose risk of injury or death – this process of asking what bad things can happen is called *Hazard Identification and Analysis*. One identifies the hazards of a system (controller overfills storage tank with toxic chemicals), then analyzes the conditions and failures that would need to occur to cause the hazard to occur, e.g. using techniques such fault tree analysis. One then formulates safety requirements for the system designed to prevent that combination of conditions and failures. This is a powerful risk-based testing strategy, helping testing to focus on high impact defects first, and is essentially what we've done in this step.

## STEP 3. COMPUTE THE PRECONDITION

All that remains now is to "turn the crank" to produce a precondition from the postcondition and invariant (see Figure 8-2).

| | |
|---|---|
| CheckAmount < GiftCardValue | Start with the invariant |
| GiftCardValue – PriceOfItem < GiftCardValue | In the expression above, substitute *CheckAmount* with its value from the postcondition. |
| -PriceOfItem < 0 | Simplify the expression above by subtracting *GiftCardValue* from both sides. |
| PriceOfItem > 0 | Flip the sign. |
| | *This is our precondition!* |

Figure 8-2 Calculating the precondition for invariant *CheckAmount < GiftCardValue*

Let's put all the pieces together and see what we have. This postcondition:

$$CheckAmount = GiftCardValue - PriceOfItem$$

..meets this invariant ( property we want to always be true ):

$$CheckAmount < GiftCardValue$$

..as long as this precondition holds:

$$PriceOfItem > 0$$

The postcondition, precondition and invariant work together as a unit, as a team. They are like parts of a complete sentence; take away one, and the full meaning is not known.

Your first reaction to the precondition we've just calculated may be something like: "But of course! Everyone *assumes* that prices are greater than zero!". Right you are. And because everyone *assumes* it, it's *just* the type of precondition easily overlooked for error testing. But in fact, it *is* a precondition for the successful computation of the refund check, and things do go awry: sign errors in coding; typing mistakes while entering prices in a database; sabotage.

## MODELING STATE CHANGE

Frequently a use case involves change to the state of a system. In such instances, in order to calculate preconditions we need a way to model the system's *before* and *after* state. Again, a simple example is the best way to illustrate. In the following example, *WidgetsInStock* is a state variable; a set of state variables such as *WidgetsInStock* are what define the state of, say, an inventory control system. We can represent the after version of a state variable with the postfix prime ( ' ). This equation describes the expected results of one step in a use case, that of shipping widgets. It describes the relationship between the number of widgets that were in stock when the use case started (no prime), versus the number of widgets in stock *after* some number were shipped (primed):

$$WidgetsInStock' = WidgetsInStock - WidgetsShipped$$

Again, keep in mind "=" is equality, not assignment: the equation describes a *relationship* between the variables.[106]

Having *before* and *after* versions of state variables allows us to talk about invariants that apply to both. The state variable *WidgetsInStock* is subject to the invariant that it should *always* be greater than or equal to zero, and this should be true *before* and *after* the postcondition completes. Here is this invariant stated for the *after* version of the state variable, i.e. this use case should *never* ship more widgets than are in stock (that's the failure to be avoided):

$$\text{Invariant: } WidgetsInStock' \geq 0$$

Turning the crank, we get the precondition that ensures the postcondition meets this invariant (see Figure 8-3).

| | |
|---|---|
| $WidgetsInStock' \geq 0$ | Start with the invariant. |
| $WidgetsInStock - WidgetsShipped$ $\geq 0$ | In the expression above, substitute *WidgetsInStock'* with its value from the postcondition. |
| $WidgetsInStock \geq WidgetsShipped$ | Simplify the expression above by adding *WidgetsShipped* to both sides. This is our precondition. |

Figure 8-3 Calculating precondition for invariant *WidgetsInStock'* $\geq 0$

---

[106] The convention used here of decorating state variables with prime follows that of the model-based specification languages Z and VDM. In Eiffel, the prefix *old* is used: *WidgetsInStock = old WidgetsInStock – WidgetsShipped*. See Bertrand Meyer, Object-Oriented Software Construction. In UML's Object Constraint Language (OCL) the postfix @pre is used: *WidgetsInStock = WidgetsInStock@pre – WidgetsShipped*. See Warmer and Kleppe, Object Constraint Language: Precise Modeling with UML.

Working through simple examples such as this allows you to gain confidence that the technique yields results you intuitively know are true.

## MODEL-BASED SPECIFICATION

Models – explicit or mental – play a big role in failure analysis, and in test design. This technique is a style of modeling aptly named *model-based specification*: it relies on building a simple model of the data and/or state of the thing being specified, then operations – e.g. steps in a use case -- are defined in terms of how they modify that model.

There is a subtle, but very important point that needs to be made about the state variables used in model-based specification, especially if you are accustomed to "instance variables" or "member variables" in object-oriented programming languages. The variables *WidgetsInStock* and *WidgetsInStock'* are two separate variables in the model we are building. They do refer to the same single instance/member variable in the application (assuming that is how the application was implemented), but it requires multiple, separate variables in the model-based specification itself in order to be able to talk about the different states the application instance/member variable might be in.

## REASONING ABOUT STATE THROUGH TIME

Working with *before* and *after* versions of state variables, unprimed and primed respectively (and remember they are separate variables in the model) can take some getting accustomed to, but it is a *powerful* technique for reasoning about use cases. It's basically the same technique physicists use when they talk about, say, the velocity of an object at *time-zero* with a variable like $V^0$, versus the velocity at *time-n* with a variable like $V^n$. Let's work through another example using this technique.

### USE CASE OVERVIEW

A manufacturing plant uses a storage tank to hold chemicals needed for its widget production; see Figure 8-4. The storage tank has a pipe in through which the chemical flows to fill the tank, and a pipe out of which the chemical flows to the machine that manufactures widgets. Rate of production by manufacturing determines the rate at which the chemical is needed, and hence the rate of flow out of the tank. A new computer based controller is being built to monitor levels in the tank, increasing or decreasing flow into the tank as needed. Sensors provide the controller with the current level in the tank, and the controller is programmed with a set target at which levels are ideally maintained in order to achieve a desired fluid pressure in the tank.

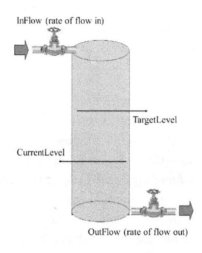

Figure 8-4 Chemical tank diagram showing flow in, and flow out of the tank

Figure 8-5 is the main scenario of the use case for maintaining the level of the chemical in the tank at the target level. The actor in this use case is the controller.

Use Case: **Maintain Chemical Level**

Controller maintains target level of chemical in tank

Main scenario

- Controller notices that chemical has dropped below target level.
- Controller increases the flow into the tank.
- Controller monitors rise of level in tank.
- When chemical reaches target level, controller reduces flow into the tank so as not to overfill the tank. Chemical is restored to target level.

Figure 8-5 Main scenario, controller's use case for maintaining level of chemical in tank

Use case description in hand, we are ready to think about how the controller might fail while executing this use case, and identify preconditions that would guard against it.

## STEP 1. FIND "RISKY" POSTCONDITIONS: MODEL AS EQUATIONS

Clearly, controlling the rate of flow into the tank is the heart of this use case, and a source of risk. Focusing on the control of this, we build a simple model of the postconditions of this facet of the use case (see Figure 8-6).

$$0 \leq InFlow \leq MaxFlow$$
$$0 \leq OutFlow \leq MaxFlow$$

A good place to start any model is to define the *domain* – the set of all possible valid values -- for the variables. Domain definitions act like invariants: they are assumed to always be true, e.g. *InFlow* should never drop below zero, or be greater than *MaxFlow*.

Lower Boundary: In this case, simply asking if *InFlow* and *OutFlow* could be negative leads to the question of direction of flow of fluid in the pipes; A negative flow would indicate backwards movement through the pipes, known as backwash. We decide this is a real possibility, but one to be covered by another use case. This use case will deal only with forward movement through the pipe.

Upper Boundary: *MaxFlow* is some upper bound that specifies the maximum *safe* rate of flow into, or out of, the tank (safe in terms of design limits on flow valves, tank construction, etc.)

InFlow$'$ = OutFlow + Delta

The first step in the use case is that the controller notices that levels are too low, and acts to increase flow into the tank to start refilling.

This postcondition describes the results of that operation: it says the flow into the tank is changed by amount *Delta*[107], causing the level to rise. Note the use of prime to distinguish the new rate of flow (primed) from the initial (unprimed).

InFlow$''$ = OutFlow$'$

At some point, the level of the chemical reaches the target level. To prevent the level from continuing to rise, the rate of flow into the tank is changed once again, this time to match the rate of flow out. This will hold the level at a steady state until such time as the flow rate out of the tank changes again. Notice the use of primes to distinguish the final rate of flow *in* (double primed) from the initial rate (unprimed) and the intermediate rate (one prime).

Notice also the use of primes to distinguish the rate of flow *out* of the tank subsequent to the start of refilling, through to the end of use case (primed)

---

[107] "Delta", the Greek letter, is often used to denote change. Here it represents the incremental increase in rate of flow into the tank used for refilling. It is a constant whose actual value the model does not specify.

versus the initial rate (unprimed); because filling the tank will take time, the rate of flow out of the tank may have changed from its initial value by the time the use case completes.

Figure 8-6 Model of main scenario for refilling chemical tank

## STEP 2. IDENTIFY A POTENTIAL FAILURE: STATE AN INVARIANT

There are two obvious failures this use case presents: failure to properly control the level resulting in the level dropping too low for manufacturing purposes, or the other extreme, overfilling the tank resulting in a chemical spill.

From these potential failures, let's identify invariants, something that should always be true about the rates of flow into, and out of, the tank for this use case.

In this use case we have identified these state variables representing the rate of flow into and out of the tank at different points in time:

> InFlow – initial rate of flow into the tank when the use case starts
> InFlow' – the flow rate to increase the level in the tank
> InFlow" – the flow rate at the end of the use case to stabilize the level
> OutFlow – initial rate of flow out of the tank when the use case starts
> OutFlow' – the rate of flow out of tank subsequent to the start of refilling, through to end of use case

For this use case, the invariants of Figure 8-7 should always be true about these state variables; if postconditions of the use case violate them, the failures identified above are possible outcomes.

| | |
|---|---|
| **Invariant: InFlow' > OutFlow** | If this were not true, the level would not rise. |
| **Invariant: InFlow" < InFlow'** | If the rate of flow is high enough to cause the level to rise (*InFlow'*), it will have to be reduced at the end of the use case scenario to prevent overfilling (*InFlow"*). Hence, *InFlow"* must be lower than *InFlow'* or overfilling will occur. In relational database lingo this is similar to what C.J. Date calls a *transition constraint*; it constrains the legal transitions of a variable from one value to another. |

Figure 8-7 Invariants that should always be true when refilling the tank

We now have a model of the postconditions and invariants they should not violate, i.e. cause to fail. We are ready to calculate preconditions needed to guard the invariants.

## STEP 3. CALCULATE PRECONDITIONS

We now calculate the precondition for each of these invariants, one at a time. Remember a precondition guards a specific invariant from one or more specific postconditions. They work as a unit. We start with *InFlow' > OutFlow* (see Figure 8-8).

| | |
|---|---|
| InFlow' > OutFlow | Start with the invariant |
| OutFlow + Delta > OutFlow | In the expression above, substitute *InFlow'* with its value from the postcondition, i.e. |
| | *InFlow'* = *OutFlow* + *Delta* |
| Delta > 0 | Solve the expression above for *Delta*. This is our precondition. |

Figure 8-8 Calculating the precondition to guard invariant *InFlow' > OutFlow*

A precondition of *Delta* > 0 is intuitive, and probably assumed. But as noted previously, assumptions are often overlooked; from a testing perspective one would want to ensure that the system checks for this case as ignoring it could eventually lead to depletion of chemicals in the tank.

Now we calculate the precondition for the next invariant, *InFlow''* < *InFlow'* (See Figure 8-9).

| | |
|---|---|
| InFlow'' < InFlow' | Start with the invariant |
| OutFlow' < OutFlow + Delta | In the expression above, substitute *InFlow'* and *InFlow''* with their values from these postconditions: |
| | *InFlow''* = *OutFlow'* |
| | *InFlow'* = *OutFlow* + *Delta* |
| | The result can't be simplified further; |
| | This is our precondition. |

Figure 8-9 Calculate precondition to guard invariant *InFlow''* < *InFlow'*

What does *OutFlow'* < *OutFlow + Delta* as a precondition mean? This precondition has identified a potentially hazardous race condition in our use case. Because filling the tank will take time, the rate of flow out of the tank may change before the target level is reached. If, during the filling of the tank, *OutFlow'* were to increase to be *equal* to *OutFlow + Delta*, the level in the tank would stop rising, stabilize, and the use case would not terminate until the flow out changed again. If during the filling of the tank *OutFlow'* were to increase to be *greater* than *OutFlow + Delta*, the level in the tank would fall, potentially depleting chemicals in the tank. This precondition has identified that for the invariant to be met, *OutFlow'* can fluctuate up or down, but *only* if it stays strictly less than *OutFlow + Delta*. Clearly such a race condition cannot be allowed and something will need to be done to prevent this, e.g. some semaphore or constraint mechanism to prevent variance in the flow out of the tank, caused by manufacturing, while the use case is in progress.

In short, this precondition has found the holy grail of test cases: a defect found before it reaches code!

## EXPLORING BOUNDARY CONDITION FAILURES

Many system failures don't show up until the system is operated at or near its boundary conditions; this is the motivation behind testing techniques such as boundary-value analysis and domain analysis for example. Let's see how we can apply model-based specification to our chemical tank use case, identifying the preconditions that specify when a system can be operated safely at its boundaries, and conversely when we can expect failures to occur.

### STEP 1. IDENTIFY POSTCONDITIONS ASSOCIATED WITH BOUNDARIES OF OPERATION

In the previous section boundaries were identified on the rate of flow in and out of the chemical tank:

$$0 \leq InFlow \leq MaxFlow$$
$$0 \leq OutFlow \leq MaxFlow$$

Now we need to identify those postconditions[108] that modify these variables, and hence have the potential of pushing the system beyond its specified bounds; in our chemical tank example we have identified these two:

InFlow' = OutFlow + Delta
InFlow" = OutFlow'

## STEP 2. STATE AN INVARIANT THE POSTCONDITIONS SHOULD NOT VIOLATE

In a model-based specification, when you define the boundaries on an initial state variable (unprimed) – in testing this is called the *domain* of the variable -- it applies not only to the initial form of the variable, i.e. *InFlow* and *OutFlow*, but also to the *primed* versions as well, *InFlow'*, *InFlow"* and *OutFlow'*. The domain definition of a variable is an invariant in its own right, one that is said to be true for all versions of the variable, primed and unprimed, in any scenario of the use case. What this means is that these boundary definitions:

0 ≤ InFlow ≤ MaxFlow
0 ≤ OutFlow ≤ MaxFlow

also imply these, which we take as invariants that we want to assure never fail:

0 ≤ InFlow' ≤ MaxFlow
0 ≤ InFlow" ≤ MaxFlow
0 ≤ OutFlow' ≤ MaxFlow

## STEP 3. CALCULATE PRECONDITIONS

What we want to determine is what additional preconditions – if any – are needed to prevent the postconditions of Step 1 from causing the invariants of Step 2 to fail.

---

[108] If you did not already have these postconditions you would look for operations and model their postconditions as equations in terms of the identified state variables.

But what did I mean by "*If any*"? When calculating preconditions, there are four possible outcomes:

- The precondition is such that it is *always* true, or said another way *there is no precondition*, meaning the postcondition should work in all circumstances (we'll see one later in the chapter; Example 3: Return Books Use Case)
- The calculated precondition is already *implied* by another existing precondition; in this event no additional precondition is needed.
- The calculated precondition is *identical* to one already noted; again no new precondition is needed.
- Or – Bingo!, we identify a missing precondition that is needed to avert failure.

The boundary statements above work out to be six separate precondition calculations: three boundary statements (*InFlow'*, *InFlow''* and *OutFlow'*) with each requiring one calculation for the lower bound, and one for the upper bound. As it turns out, of the six calculated preconditions, five are either implied or equal to existing preconditions. For brevity's sake we won't do those calculations here. But one boundary does in fact identify a failure scenario, and we calculate the precondition needed to guard against it in Figure 8-10.

| | |
|---|---|
| InFlow' ≤ MaxFlow | Start with the invariant |
| OutFlow + Delta ≤ MaxFlow | In the expression above, substitute *InFlow'* with its value from the postcondition, i.e. *InFlow'* = *OutFlow* + *Delta* |
| OutFlow ≤ MaxFlow – Delta | Solve for *OutFlow*. |
| | This is our precondition. |

Figure 8-10 Calculating precondition to guard invariant *InFlow'* ≤ *MaxFlow*

The failure scenario we have identified is this. If at the start of the use case, the flow *out* of the tank is running at maximum, i.e. *OutFlow = MaxFlow*, it will not be possible to increase the flow into the tank high enough to start refilling the tank without setting *InFlow'* to a value *higher* than *MaxFlow*, the upper bound on safe rate of flow in and out of the tank. The precondition states the use case can only be expected to work if *OutFlow* is *less than maximum* when the use case starts. As we have already established *Delta > 0*, we know *OutFlow will* be less than the maximum in the precondition.

Notice also that this precondition is a stronger constraint than the original domain definition, i.e. the new precondition *OutFlow ≤ MaxFlow − Delta implies* the domain definition condition of *OutFlow <= MaxFlow*, but not vice versa, so the former is said to be the *stronger* condition, and the latter the *weaker*. In effect, the stronger overrides the weaker.

## EXTENDING MODEL-BASED SPECIFICATION TO USE SETS

To this point in the chapter all examples presented on calculating preconditions have been numeric in nature; use cases that have numeric aspects such as money, numbers of widgets in stock, rates of flow of chemicals, etc..

Numeric problems provide a big "bang for the buck" in the application of model-based specification. First, there are many problems that can be stated numerically; after all, numerical computation is the birthplace of computing. Most applications, even if not predominantly numerically oriented, are likely to have some component that *is* numeric in nature. And applying this technique to numeric models is as easy as it gets, requiring little more than simple algebra.

But model-based specification and calculated preconditions are certainly not limited to numeric applications and next we'll look at applying this technique to use case operations that can be modeled with *sets*, which is the foundation for such model-based specification languages such as Z. Doing so greatly broadens the scope of applications to which we can apply this technique for use case failure analysis.

No background in set theory is assumed and we'll cover the basics here. If you want to dive a bit deeper into set theory for testers, Jorgensen's chapter, Discrete Math for Testers, would be a good reference.[109]

## *A FEW SIMPLES THINGS TO KEEP IN MIND ABOUT "SETS"*

A "set" is a collection of things. Amazing to think that something so low-tech sounding could be the basis for things such as modern mathematics and database theory! But indeed sets are powerful tool for modeling.

If your set theory is a little rusty, here's a few, simple things to keep in mind about sets for modeling. First, in modeling with sets you are usually building a set of "things" of the same type: a set of employees in a company; a set of bank accounts. The elements of a set can also be types themselves, e.g. the kinds of animals at your local zoo: elephants, tigers, giraffes, bears and so on. Each of those could in turn have a corresponding set that lists names of the actual animals at your zoo, e.g. Smoky might be in the set of bears at your zoo. The act of identifying and categorizing things into sets by type is actually part of the analysis that takes place through modeling.

Second, there are no duplicate elements in a set. When you model something as a set you are making a claim that this property of sets applies to the thing being modeled. So modeling a bank's account numbers as a set implies you don't expect for there to be two accounts with the same account number. The significance of this property of sets will be clearer when we get to our example.[110]

Third, one of the properties about sets we often want to talk about in modeling is the number of things – the elements – in the set; this is called the *cardinality* of a set. A set with no elements is called the empty set or null set; its cardinality is zero. Some sets even have an infinite number of elements, e.g. the set of integers.

---

[109] Paul Jorgensen, *Software Testing: A Craftsman's Approach*
[110] If you need to model a collection of things that allows for duplicates that's a "bag" and recognizing that something has that property is part of the modeling. We won't talk about bags here but they would also be a nice next-step addition to the tool kit; if you are using both in your model you just need to keep straight which things are being modeled with sets and which are being modeled as bags.

And finally, as with numbers, there are ways to "add", "subtract" and compare sets (e.g. Are these sets equal? Are there common elements in these sets?).

A good next step up from applying model-based specification to the numeric parts of use cases is applying it those aspects of use cases that can be modeled using these simple properties of sets. Adding simple sets to your modeling toolkit broadens the things in use cases you can model, but without making things too complicated. And because cardinality – the number of elements in the set - is itself a numeric value it allows you to re-use what you've already learned about calculating numeric preconditions  from the previous chapter.

Let's return to our library management system for an example.

## EXAMPLE 1: MODEL BASED SPECIFICATION WITH SETS

Recall that one of the actors in the library management system is the Self Service Kiosk. Not a person, but rather a new kiosk system the library is trying for select library users with special library cards. The Self Service Kiosk allows these special users to lend and return books themselves without the assistance of a librarian (refer back to use case diagram of Figure 1-7).

Let's assume we have identified the need for a new use case to help determine usage patterns for the new kiosks. Once a month, a book curator (another actor in the use case diagram of Figure 1-7) downloads to a master database a report of kiosk activity for that month. Each kiosk has a small amount of memory used to store a month's worth of data, and an internal clock time stamps each day's activity. But curators want to be able to look at usage trends over longer than a month, so a new master database will be created to hold cumulative data allowing curators to run reports on daily usage patterns over many years.

The basic flow of the new use case is shown in Figure 8-11.

Curator downloads to database a report of kiosk activity for that month.

Basic Flow

- Book curator logs into library master database with ID and password.
- Curator navigates to reporting page and clicks on link titled download kiosk activity data. A transfer of data from kiosk's memory to the master database is initiated. Activities for new dates are added to database.
- When transfer is complete, curator is prompted as to whether kiosk memory should be cleared. Curator responds yes, then logs off.

Figure 8-11 Basic flow for use case Download Kiosk Activity Data

What we want to do now is think about how a system implementing this use case might fail. To do this, we'll build a simple model of a risky operation using sets. In doing so we'll be looking for that "Ah HA!" insight into the operation; that moment when we say "Hmm, hadn't really thought about that happening before.."

## Step1. Model Postcondition of Risky Operation

As discussed before in this chapter (see Step 1. Find A "Risky" Postcondition: Model As An Equation), a good first step is simply to model the postcondition of some operation we are concerned about. In our example, let's focus on step 2 of the use case. When this operation completes, the master database has been updated to include the activity recorded for all the dates stored in the kiosk memory.

So let's write a simple post condition, using sets as our modeling tool, for the expected results of this operation.

Remember that one of the things you can do to sets is "add" them together, called set *union*; shown as ∪. Let's say *Dates* is the set of dates that the master database has data for and *NewDates*? is the set dates to be downloaded to the database for the week. We might have a postcondition like:

$$Dates' = Dates \cup NewDates?$$

194

In words the postcondition says that the expected result of the operation of step 2 is that *Dates'* will be equal to the old values of *Dates* plus the elements of *NewDates?* "added" in. And keep in mind that when you take the union of sets, the result is a set itself, with no duplicate elements.

Notice the "?" at the end of the set *NewDates?*; This wasn't discussed before, but the postfix "?" is used to represent an input, as opposed to a state variable. *NewDates?* is an input to the use case and is the set of new dates for which chemical data is being recorded this week. Inputs and outputs to the use case are transient; not part of the state and modeling wise it's often a good idea to make that specific.[111]

## Step 2. State an Invariant

Next we state some invariant; something that should always be true about this postcondition. Recall from the previous chapter, invariants are to postconditions what safety requirements are to safety critical systems: a statement – a *cross-check* – of what a "safe" postcondition looks like.

For the invariant we need a way to talk about the number of elements in a set. For this we have the symbol "#"[112]. The prefix # means cardinality of a set; the number of elements in a set. For example #{} = 0 and #{a,b,c} = 3. So how about this invariant:

$$\#Dates' = \#Dates + \#NewDates?$$

In words, after the completion of the operation of step 2, we expect that the number of dates for which there is data (*#Dates'*) to be equal to the number of dates before the download (*#Dates*), plus the number of dates downloaded for that week (*#NewDates?*).

Sounds pretty straightforward. How could it fail?

--------

[111] The postfix "?" is borrowed from the specification language Z (pronounced "Zed"). Outputs in Z have the postfix "!"
[112] Again, borrowed from the specification language Z.

## Step 3. Calculate Precondition

Next we calculate the precondition for the postcondition that is needed (if any) to preserve the invariant. To do this, in the invariant we simply substitute *Dates'* with its value from the postcondition:

### Step 3a: #(Dates ∪ NewDates?) = #Dates + #NewDates?

This is actually a precondition at this point, but of course it would be good to have this in a simpler form; We might not get an "Ah HA!" moment from an expression like this.

There is an algebra for sets, just like there is an algebra for numbers or Boolean expressions. So in the following we'll use a little algebra of sets, and a little numeric algebra to simplify the expression (later in the chapter we'll be seeing a way to calculate the precondition without the algebra, but for now let's do this to illustrate the concepts covered earlier in the chapter still apply).

For two sets A and B, the following algebraic rule holds for sets:

### #( A ∪ B) = #A + #B - #(A ∩ B)

Again, if you are a little rusty on your set theory, remember that this symbol ∩ is set intersection: it "returns" all elements that are *common* to both sets; their overlap. In words, the rule simply says the cardinality of the union of two sets is the same as the sum of the cardinality of the two sets individually, but with the number of overlapping elements removed, so that overlapping elements are not counted twice.

So we can use this rule to rewrite the left side of STEP 3a above like:

### Step 3b:

#Dates + #NewDates? - # (Dates ∩ NewDates?) =
#Dates + #NewDates?

Finally, since *#Dates* + *#NewDates?* is a numeric value we can subtract it from both sides which reduces Step 3b to:

## Step3c: #(Dates ∩ NewDates?) = 0

STEP 3c is the final precondition.

What does this mean? From the perspective of the model, it means that any overlap in the two sets is not allowed. But – and this is a key part in the search for an "Ah HA!" -- in the spirit of use case failure analysis what we really want to know is what does this precondition mean *in terms of the application itself*; What might "overlap" mean in the real world application *and how might it occur*? This is truly a case where the role of modeling is to pose sharp questions about potential ways a system, specified by a use case, might fail.

Let's brainstorm for a situation where this might come about. Well, what if the kiosk clock were to be set incorrectly – backwards -- to a date for which data had already been recorded in the database. At the time of the download of new data, the curator would download data time stamped incorrectly overwriting old, already existing data: i.e. there would be some dates in *NewDates?* that were also in *Dates* already.

So to translate the model's precondition into one for the application we might say :

Precondition for main flow scenario: *"Starting range of dates downloaded from the kiosk must be later than the last date recorded in the master database".*

Modeling at even this crude level provides a way to systematically ask the right questions that let us stumble into the ways a system might fail. And that really is the goal in building a model and calculating a precondition: to have an "Ah Ha!" moment, where you step back and say "Hmm .. hadn't thought about *that* happening."

## EXAMPLE 2 CALCULATING PRECONDITIONS USING VENN DIAGRAMS

Using the algebra of numbers for calculating preconditions I can deal with pretty well. But dealing with algebraic expressions of sets can be a bit tougher; not always as intuitive. Even in the previous example we relied a bit on the algebra of numbers to help calculate the final precondition.

Wouldn't it be great if we had a way to graphically approach the problem of identifying preconditions when the model uses sets. Well, we do .. Venn diagrams!

Venn diagrams are named after logician John Venn who formalized and popularized their use in the late 1800s and are a great tool for solving problems in the algebra of sets. I'll make the assumption here that you are already familiar with Venn diagrams. If you are not, there are many, many resources describing them. What we'll focus on here is their application to the calculation of preconditions from a model based specification of an operation.[113]

Let's revisit the example just worked (Example 1: Model Based Specification with Sets) and see how to use a Venn diagram to help calculate the precondition.

## Step 1. Write Postcondition
As before, our process of specifying a postcondition remains the same.

Dates' = Dates ∪ NewDates?

## Step 2. State an Invariant
This time we'd like to state an invariant without the use of numbers (we did that last time to leverage what we already knew about calculating preconditions for numeric quantities). To do so we need to introduce a new operator for sets: "\", in words it's called *set difference*.[114] For two sets A and B, set difference is written like A \ B. Set difference returns all elements of set A with all elements of B removed. Set difference is like subtraction for sets. How about this invariant:

Dates' \ NewDates? = Dates

------

[113] Later, in section Return Books Use Case: "Blue Collar" Venn Diagram Approach, we'll see that Venn diagrams are, in general, a great brain storming tool for testers.
[114] In set theory also called "relative complement". This too is part of the specification language Z.

This invariant is basically the inverse operation of the postcondition. Same idea as "checking your answer" when doing arithmetic; apply the inverse of an arithmetic operation and you should arrive back at the number you started with.

## Step 3. Calculate Precondition using Venn Diagram

Now we are ready to calculate the precondition for this invariant. The first step is just like with numeric problems: in the invariant, replace *Dates'* with its value from the postcondition:

Initial Precondition: (Dates ∪ NewDates?) \ NewDates? = Dates

What we'll do differently now however is to use Venn diagrams to help simply this precondition in hopes of yielding something that provides that "Ah Ha!" moment, where you step back and say "Hmm .. hadn't thought about *that* happening."

And of course we already know what the "Ah Ha!" insight is from having just worked it; the point here is to simply show a much easier (in my opinion, and I bet yours as well) way to get there with a Venn diagram.

We begin by drawing a couple of Venn diagrams as shown in Figure 8-12, one for the precondition's left side (top), one for the right (bottom). For each diagram we label one circle *Dates*; this is the dates for which the master database already has information stored. The other circle we label *NewDates?*, the input to the use case which is the set of dates for which activity is being downloaded from the kiosk. The larger box in which the circles appear represents the universe of all dates.

There are two approaches to labeling the regions of a Venn diagram; one common today is to indicate what an expression includes. But Venn used a labeling scheme that noted which regions of the diagram are *excluded*, i.e. which regions are empty.[115] For this example we'll follow Venn's lead and label the regions of each Venn diagram – left and right side of precondition's equation – to show what is excluded. We'll do this by placing the empty-set symbol in regions that are excluded by the precondition; i.e. the regions are empty.

---

[115] John Venn, Symbolic Logic, 1881, p.112.

*Graph Left and Right Sides of Equation*

First we graph the left side of the precondition; this is shown in the top Venn diagram of Figure 8-12:

### Left side: (Dates U NewDates?) \ NewDates?

Next we graph the right side of the precondition; this is shown in the bottom Venn diagram of Figure 8-12:

### Right side: Dates

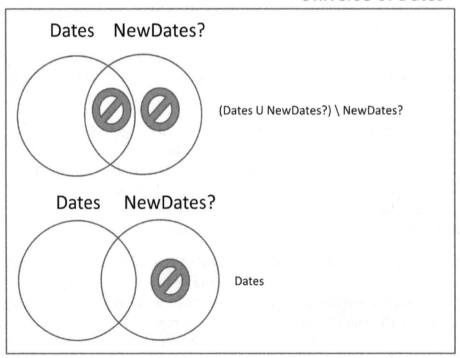

Figure 8-12 Venn diagrams for the left (top) and right (bottom) side of precondition. Regions with the empty-set symbol are excluded by the precondition; they are empty.

*Compare Venn Diagrams, Left and Right Side*

Now we compare the top and bottom diagrams of Figure 8-12. While the equation says the two should be the same, they obviously don't *look* the same; in the top diagram the "lens" between *Dates* and New*Dates?* is excluded, while in the bottom it is not.

To identify the precondition we then simply ask: Are there additional conditions under which the two diagrams would in fact *be* the same? And the answer is yes, if we assume there is no overlap (intersection) between *Dates* and *New Dates?* the two Venn diagrams would be equivalent. That additional "condition" is our final precondition, shown below:

### Final precondition: Dates ∩ NewDates? = {}

This jives with the final precondition calculated in the previous example (Example 1: Model Based Specification with Sets); i.e. the number of elements in the intersection of *Dates* and *NewDates?* needs to be zero:

### #(Dates ∩ NewDates?) = 0

I think what you'll find is that simply the act of modeling a postcondition with sets and Venn diagrams is often enough to get the mental juices going and the preconditions – and other questions pertinent to testing -- will come quite intuitively without going through the process of stating an invariant.

For example, in the Venn diagram of Figure 8-12, what does the area inside the box, but outside the two circles represent? It is dates which are "out of scope" for storage in the master database, or the kiosk tracking. Is it an empty set? If so, then all possible dates are in scope for testing? Do we need to test for dates many, many years in the past and the future? How far into the past or future is "many".

If on the other hand it's *not* an empty set, then there is apparently a bound on the past and or future dates? And once we have established bounds, we now have a means for boundary value tests, both valid and invalid.

Remember Y2K?

*EXAMPLE 3: RETURN BOOKS USE CASE*

To make sure we have a handle on using Venn diagrams in calculating preconditions, let's do another example.

At the beginning of the book we looked at an overall strategy for where and when to apply various testing techniques as illustrated in Figure 0-4. By that strategy, more rigorous techniques like model-based specification and working with preconditions is reserved for risky operations of high priority use cases.

In Chapter 2, From Use Case Diagram to Operational Profile, we looked at a Pareto chart for our public library book management system (see Figure 2-2) and found that over *90% of the activity* is accounted for by just three use cases: **Do Book Search**, **Lend Books**, and **Return Books**.

In previous chapters we've used the **Do Book Search** use case as an example for various testing techniques. Let's now turn to one of the other high frequency use cases: **Return Books** use case.

To recap, the **Return Books** use case describes the return of a checked out book or books. It assumes physical copies of one or more books is being returned. The previously created check out request is updated to show the book or books has been returned. In addition, a check is made of pending reservation requests for this book; if one exists (next in line for the book if there are multiple), the reservation is flagged to notify the person reserving the book.

We decide that a key bit of this use case from a failure analysis standpoint is the accounting which must go on to keep track of what books are currently available in the library versus what books are currently on loan. To model this, we use three sets:

> Available - the set of books available for check out in the library
> Lent - the set of books currently on loan in the library system
> Returns? -- the set of books being returned; an input to the use case

## Step 1. Model Postconditions of Risky Operation

The key accounting operation that must go on as part of the returned book use case is simply described with these postconditions. In words, when the books are returned, we need update the set of available books to show the addition of the returned books, and also update the set of books that are on loan to reflect the return of the books. Our postconditions:

Available' = Available ∪ Returned?
Lent' = Lent \ Returned?

## Step 2. State an Invariant

Now let's state an invariant for these postconditions. From a book accounting standpoint we want to make sure that books are either available for loan, or already on loan, but never both! These invariants will do the trick; in words, both before and after completion of the operation that actually checks the book back in, there should be no overlap between the set of books showing as available, and the set of books currently on loan.

Invariant before operation: Available ∩ Lent = {}
Invariant after operation: Available' ∩ Lent' = {}

## Step 3. Calculate the Precondition

To calculate the initial precondition, in the post operation invariant we substitute *Available'* and *Lent'* with their values from the postcondition:

Initial precondition:
(Available ∪ Returned?) ∩ (Lent \ Returned?) = {}

*Graph Left & Right Sides of Equation*
We now draw a Venn diagram with three circles with labels *Available*, *Lent* and *Returned?*. The three circles are inside a box the represents the universe of books in the library. This is illustrated in Figure 8-13.

# Universe of Books in Library

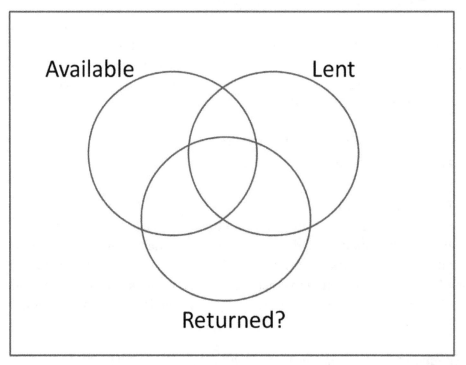

Figure 8-13 Venn diagram representing the three sets being used to model the postconditions of Return Books use case.

As in our previous example (Example 2 Calculating Preconditions Using Venn Diagrams) we now want to use the Venn diagram to visually compare the left and right sides of the initial precondition. We noted in the previous example there are two approaches to labeling the regions of a Venn diagram. In that example we followed Venn's convention of labeling regions that were *excluded* by an expression. For this example let's use the convention of shading regions of the diagram that are *included*, i.e. described by an expression. This provides us with additional flexibility; for different problems you may find one easier to use than other, and this is an approach commonly seen with Venn diagrams today.

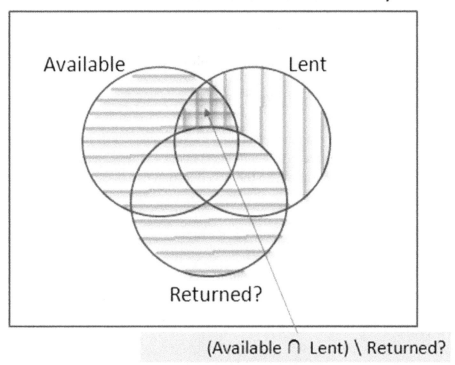

Figure 8-14 Cross hatched region that must be empty for precondition to be true.

In Figure 8-14, the left side of the precondition is depicted in Venn diagram form. The right side is just the empty set, so we don't really need to shade anything for that.

Horizontal bars are used to shade in that part of the Venn diagram that corresponds to (*Available* ∪ *Returned?*). Vertical bars shade in that part of the Venn diagram that corresponds to (*Lent* \ *Returned?*). The cross hatched area where they intersect is the bit we are interested in, the left side of the precondition (*Available* ∪ *Returned?*) ∩ (*Lent* \ *Returned?*).

*Compare Equations Left and Right Sides in Venn Diagram*
The hatched area of Figure 8-14 represents the left side of the precondition. The right side of the precondition is simply the empty set. So, for the invariant to hold, this region must be nil, or the empty set. The region can be more simply described as (*Available* ∩ *Lent*) \ *Returned?*, so this is our simplified precondition:

$$\text{(Available} \cap \text{Lent) \textbackslash Returned?} = \{\}$$

See how we are using the Venn diagram to simplify expressions? Much easier than trying to do it algebraically. And as you recall, (*Available* ∩ *Lent*) = {} was an invariant we assumed to hold before the operation. So the precondition can be simplified even more to:

$$\{\} \textbackslash \text{ Returned?} = \{\}$$

And it should be obvious that nothing (the empty set) "take away" anything is always the empty set. The final, simplified precondition is

$$\{\} = \{\}$$

This is what is called a tautology; the precondition is always true, or if you prefer, there is no precondition! The postcondition as described meets the stated invariant without a precondition.

*But is There More to the Story?*
We just saw how to use our Venn diagram to show that these postconditions:

$$\text{Available' = Available} \cup \text{Returned?}$$
$$\text{Lent' = Lent \textbackslash Returned?}$$

.. preserve this invariant:

$$\text{Available} \cap \text{Lent} = \{\}$$

.. given this precondition:

$$(\text{Available} \cap \text{Lent}) \setminus \text{Returned?} = \{\}$$

And because the invariant itself said *(Available ∩ Lent)* = {} we knew that *(Available ∩ Lent) \ Returned?* must = {} too. End of story. All is well.

But wait. If we let the picture of the Venn diagram guide us, we might notice something looks a little odd about our precondition, yielding one of those moments where you go *"Ah HA! I hadn't really thought about that"*.

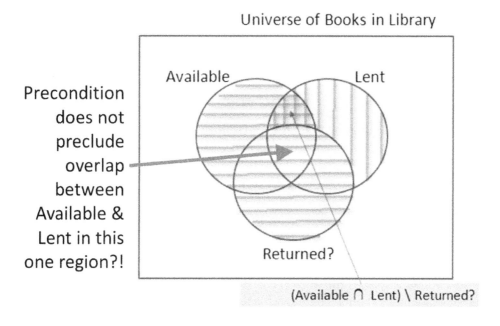

Figure 8-15 Is there something odd about the precondition?

Let's revisit our Venn diagram from Figure 8-14 reshown here as Figure 8-15. If we look at what the diagram is showing it says the precondition requires only that the hatched area be empty. But what about that region directly below, the region which represents books that are showing as *both* available and lent. Surely that must be empty also?! Well yes it should, and that is in fact what our global invariant says: no overlap is permitted between books that are available and those that are already lent. But what we've discovered is that for this operation, we can actually get by with a precondition that is weaker; *just* the hatched area needs to be nil.

This should be an alarm that something more may be going on, and that we need to spend some time asking *why* this is so. Here's the failure scenario identified. If at the start of the operation we have books being returned that are mistakenly shown by the system as both available *and* simultaneously already lent, and if we don't check this fact before the operation begins, the operation's actions as described by the postconditions could well (depending on how the code implements the operation) "fix" the accounting problem as it updates the books. The operation could *overwrite* the returned books' status to the correct settings: available, not lent.

Remember back in Figure 4-5 we discussed how separate faults can sometimes interact in such a way as to mask one another? This is a similar situation where code execution could well mask the presence of the fault, in this case actually fixing the book accounting mistake, but of course not fixing the problem that injected the fault in the first place. The fault goes undetected to surface as a defect another time.

This is the beauty of modeling, getting the mental juices going, helping spot things we might otherwise miss. And this is especially the beauty of what has made Venn diagrams so popular from day one: the ability to spot things *visually* that might otherwise allude our eye amongst a lot of complicated math.

## WORKING SMART IN HOW YOU APPLY WHAT YOU'VE LEARNED

Mathematically based techniques like model-based specification are called formal methods. As with any rigorous technique, you might not want to apply it to *every* use case.

Prioritize where you apply model-based specification. The operational profiles discussed in Chapter 2 and Chapter 4 let you know which use cases will be frequently used, and of those, which scenarios (paths through a particular use case) will be frequently trafficked. One then can focus on modeling the operations of a scenario most critical.

A good approach to applying this technique would be to triage use cases based on risk exposure – a function of frequency and severity of failure – and apply it to high risk use cases. A low-tech, visual approach to the triage of use cases is a "Boston Matrix" with the horizontal axis representing frequency of use, and vertical axis representing use case criticality (see Figure 8-16). Each use case is assigned to one of four quadrants, high-risk use cases receiving the most attention. The upper right quadrant represents those use cases that are both frequently used, and critical in nature, and where the biggest bang for the buck from applying failure analysis via model-based specification will come from.

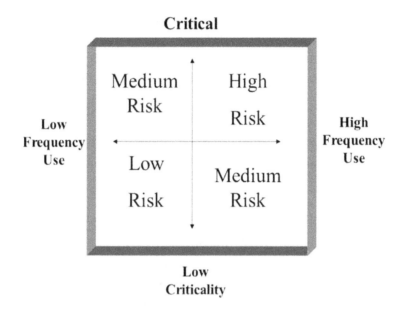

Figure 8-16 Boston Matrix style approach to triaging use cases based on frequency of use and criticality.

## THE LEAST YOU NEED TO KNOW ABOUT PRECONDITIONS, POSTCONDITIONS AND INVARIANTS

If prior to reading this book your only exposure to preconditions and postconditions has been via the use case literature, then this chapter may be a bit like – as they say – "drinking from a fire hose". So if you are thinking this is way too complicated, let me leave you with *one fundamental lesson and three simple rules* that anyone can use on absolutely any use case anytime. Period.

As I noted previously, mathematically based techniques like this are called formal methods. I coined the term *"blue collar formal methods"* to capture the idea that for many formal methods – e.g. model-based specification -- there is often a less rigorous application of the method that provides benefit without necessarily getting into all the math. It's like there is a *fundamental lesson* to be learned from the formal method, but once learned you can use that lesson without the math itself.

What would a "blue collar" version of this technique look like? Do you remember that at the start of this chapter I made the comment *"If you look at your favorite book on use cases you are likely to find use cases with preconditions, but no postconditions (the significance of which will make sense later) .."*. Do you see the significance now? If preconditions are calculated from a postcondition to preserve an invariant, what sense does it make to have a precondition *without* a postcondition or an invariant?!

Here then is the fundamental lesson that model-based specification teaches:

*Preconditions, postconditions and invariants work as a team. They travel as a trio. If you see one without the others, something is missing! Remember, the team that plays together stays together.*

Here are three simple rules for applying that fundamental lesson:

1. When you write or see a lone precondition for a use case your first thought should be, "Hmm .. I wonder what happens if it fails?". Ask yourself what postcondition it is associated with and what hazard (violated invariant) it prevents the postcondition from causing. Yes, you intuitively know that precondition is needed, but take some time to try and identify *why* it's needed and the *consequence* of its failure. Remember: the precondition is part of a trio; find the rest of the team.
2. Postconditions are where the action is at in the use case, describing the output produced and state changed. And it is precisely when you are generating outputs and changing state that bad things can happen. When you write or see a lone postcondition, ask yourself "I wonder what hazard this postcondition poses (violated invariant) and what precondition could prevent it?" Think *team*. Think *trio*.
3. Start thinking in terms of *what must always be true about a use case*, i.e. its' invariants. A good way to identify invariants is to think about what can go wrong -- *hazard identification* -- then work backwards from the hazard to identify what needs to stay right to prevent it. And once you have an

210

invariant look for operations whose postconditions could violate it, then see rule #2.

Finally I would add that for failure analysis and test design these rules need to be applied at the operation level, i.e. to the individual steps that make up the use case.

## CHAPTER REVIEW

Let's review the key points from this chapter. Model-based specification is a technique for crisply specifying the expected behavior of use case operations. Its components – a simplified model of inputs, outputs and state; preconditions; postconditions *and invariants* – provide an integrated basis for use case failure analysis and test design.

Preconditions, postconditions and invariants *work as a team*. The precondition identifies the conditions under which a postcondition – which describes the results of a use case operation – will work correctly, and not cause the invariant to fail.

Invariants are to use cases what safety requirements are to safety critical systems. They are a statement of properties about the use case that we expect to be true. A good way to identify invariants is to identify potential hazards of the use case, then work backwards to identify what must be true to prevent the hazard.

A technique exists for the calculation of preconditions from a postcondition and invariant. For numeric applications the technique requires little more than simple algebra. For models based on sets, Venn diagrams are very useful.

Each operation or step that makes up a use case can have preconditions which describe the conditions under which that operation will work, and postconditions that describe outputs and state change of the operation. These operation preconditions and postconditions are the source of preconditions and postconditions that the use case literature associates with the use case as a whole.

# Chapter 9 BRAINSTORMING TESTS: MODELING WITH RELATIONS

In the previous chapter I noted that models – explicit or mental – play a big role in failure analysis, and in test design. *Model-based specification* languages such as Z rely on building a simple model of the data and/or state of the thing being specified, then operations – i.e. steps in a use case -- are defined in terms of how they modify that model via postconditions [116].

That chapter began with numeric models as a simple basis to illustrate the important connection between preconditions, postconditions and invariants. The chapter concluded by expanding the modeling tool kit to include sets.

In this chapter we extend the modeling tool kit to include relations between sets. Boris Beizer, in his book Black-Box Testing, has a section called Living and Working with Relations in which he makes the comment *"Relations have properties and therefore can be categorized. If you can say 'Oh! This is such-and-such a kind of relation,' then whatever you know about that kind of relation in general applies to the specific case"*.

That comment pretty well sums the heart of this chapter.

In the previous chapter we have been discussing how to *calculate* preconditions, and more generally the special relationship between preconditions, postconditions and invariants. The precondition identifies the conditions under which a postcondition – which describes the results of a use case operation – will work correctly, and not cause the invariant to fail.

As you might guess, by adding relations to the tester's modeling tool kit, calculation of preconditions only gets harder.

---

[116] See Binder, *Testing Object-Oriented Systems*, Part II, Models, for a broader discussion of the role of models in testing.

But there is hope for the test practitioner! In this chapter we'll look at ways to use models built from sets and relations to help spot preconditions without actually going through the formalization of *calculating* the precondition. More generally we'll find that these models are a good way to brainstorm tests in general for a use case operation.

This is another instance of what I called in the last chapter "blue collar formal methods". Once you understand the fundamental lesson to be learned from a formal method such as calculating the precondition, you might find less rigorous applications of a method that provides benefit without necessarily getting into all the math.

## TESTABLE PROPERTIES OF SETS

Before diving into relations over sets, let's first do a refresher on the testable properties of sets themselves. The simplest data model we can build from sets is simply to say that something is a set! In doing so we are making the claim that that thing has the properties of a set.

In the last chapter, we looked at some basic properties of sets (see A Few Simples Things to Keep In Mind about "Sets"):

- There are *no duplicate elements in a set*. When you model something as a set you are making a claim that this property of sets applies to the thing being modeled.
- Another property of sets is its *cardinality:* the number of things – the elements – in the set. A set with no elements is called the empty set or null set; its cardinality is zero. Some sets even have an infinite number of elements, e.g. the set of integers.

Both of these properties are *testable*. By simply claiming that a thing is a set, we have identified test cases we might want to consider: Given a set does not allow for duplicate elements, what happens if we try to add an element already in the set? E.g. in our library system the set of  ISBN numbers for books in the library is a set. We should never be allowed to add a new book title with the same ISBN number of another book.

And the cardinality of a set as a number is amenable to boundary value testing, i.e. the fewest number of elements we expect in the set, and the largest number of elements.

OK, we're now ready to dive into brainstorming tests from relations over sets. Venn diagrams are a good place to begin.

## RETURN BOOKS USE CASE: VENN DIAGRAM BRAINSTORMING

Remember in the last two examples from the previous chapter (Example 2 Calculating Preconditions Using Venn Diagrams, Example 3: Return Books Use Case) we saw how Venn diagrams could be used to calculate preconditions from a postcondition and invariant.

Well, Venn diagrams are one way of expressing relations between sets. In addition to being a handy way to calculate the precondition for a specific postcondition and invariant, they turn out to be a great tool for simply *brainstorming* tests.

Let's back up and take a second look at the last example from the last chapter (Example 3: Return Books Use Case) and see how we could have used a Venn diagram to brainstorm tests for that use case.

Our brainstorming approach still involves a test model, and we'll use the same one we used previously, recapped here.

As you'll recall, the **Return Books** use case describes the return of a checked out book or books. A key bit of this use case from a failure analysis standpoint is the accounting which must go on to keep track of what books are currently available in the library versus what books are currently on loan. To model this, we used three sets:

> Available - the set of books available for check out in the library
> Lent - the set of books currently on loan in the library system
> Returns? - the set of books being returned; an input to the use case

The actual return operation was then described with these postconditions:

Available' = Available ∪ Returned?
Lent' = Lent \ Returned?

Now however, we dispense with the calculation of the precondition, and rather simply build a Venn diagram of the postconditions' *starting* state variables (unprimed) and use case input, and use the Venn diagram as a brainstorming "checklist" to help us intuitively spot preconditions and other test design issues in general.

## Universe of Books in Library

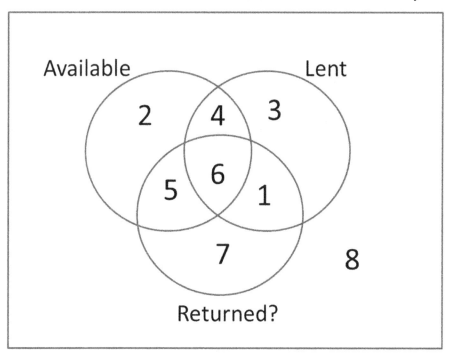

Figure 9-1 Venn diagram for brainstorming tests for the Return Books use case

Figure 9-1 is a Venn diagram for the starting state variables (*Available*, *Lent*) and input (*Returned?*) used in the postconditions. Each region of the Venn diagram has been numbered. *These regions represent eight questions we should ask ourselves about our use case operation*, i.e. what does each of the eight regions represent about the **Return Books** use case operation? The act of working through what these regions represent is a great way to gain a deeper understanding of the problem and brainstorm preconditions, invariants and failure scenarios.

Let's walk through each region.

### REGION 1

Region 1 is some subset of books that are lent that are being returned. You might think of this as the "happy path" region of the diagram. The books being returned are properly lent and are not showing as available.

Even at this early stage you are probably getting an idea of the power of what we are doing here. If only *one* of eight regions represents the "happy path", do some of the other seven represent ways things could go wrong with the use case?!

### REGIONS 2, 3 AND 4

Regions 2 and 3 represent books that are available or lent, respectively, and are not part of the return. But what's that region 4 where the Available and Lent circles overlap? These are books that for some reason are showing as *both* available and lent. While not part of the books being returned, this region reminds us of an important *global invariant* that should *always* be true: *books should appear as either available, or lent, but never both*, i.e. region 4 should be empty in our Venn diagram.

This is the same invariant we used previously to calculate the precondition for this operation's postconditions (previous chapter, Example 3: Return Books Use Case).

$$\text{Available} \cap \text{Lent} = \{\}$$

It should be reassuring that the Venn diagram has provided us a way to systematically ask the right question that would lead to that invariant.

This invariant is a *global invariant*. Global invariants are ones that are true for all states of a system, and as they apply to use cases, they are true for all scenarios of the use case, and probably for all use cases of the system.[117]

Global invariants are in a sense, *preconditions on steroids*. Whereas a "regular" precondition may only guard one specific postcondition, global invariants act as guards to *all* postconditions that use the state variables covered in the global invariant. From a failure analysis and testing perspective it is useful to keep this point in mind as they provide additional ways to validate the correct functioning of the system. *A global invariant is a mini test case that can be repeated over and over to reaffirm that property of the system is still holding.* It should be true before an operation, and after.

## REGIONS 5 AND 6

Region 5 represents a case where the books being returned are showing as *already available, and not currently lent*! How could that happen? Were they stolen and are now being returned? Or did the books' status not get correctly registered when the books were lent? Were the books somehow mistakenly marked as returned and available before hand when they should not have been? Region 5 should be empty in our Venn diagram and represents a failure scenario of the use case which may need to be tested.

Region 6 represents a case where the returned books are a subset of those lent (as they should be), but somehow are also showing as available! Clearly something has gone wrong. Again, region 6 should be empty and represents a failure scenario of the use case.

Looking at both regions 5 and 6, a reasonable *global invariant* (and hence precondition) would seem to be: Returned books should show as having been lent, and *not* available. If this invariant is false before the operation begins, the system

---

[117] A common type of global invariant is the *data invariant*, which expresses some property that is true about data in the system. They are variously called *state invariants* when used with state variables, and *class invariants* when used in the context of classes. I use the term global invariant as that is less implementation specific, and makes clear its global versus local nature.

should flag the problem. Steps would need to be taken (say by a library system administrator) to distinguish between the two cases outlined for regions 5 and 6, and pinpoint and correct the problem (e.g. is there a bug in the system that allows for ambiguous status). A test case for region 5 would, in particular, be straightforward to test for: attempt to return a book that was not checked out.

Do you see how this is working? In working through the regions we identify failure scenarios (e.g. books being returned that are showing as being available and never lent), in which case we then brainstorm ways that failure scenario could happen, along with tests to show that the system is capable of preventing or detecting (say via operation precondition checks) those failure scenarios.

### REGIONS 7 AND 8

The regions so far, 1 through 6, have dealt with books that are available or lent, and were contained within the Venn circles of the same names. Regions 7 and 8 are those regions outside the Available or Lent circles. What types or status of books might there be besides available or lent? One possibility is non-circulating, books which must be read in the library, and cannot be checked out. Libraries categorize some books non-circulating for various reasons. High use books, like reference books, can be set aside for use in the library only; fragile, rare books or manuscripts are often categorized non-circulating to protect them from wear and to supervise their use. A library may also have books made completely unavailable for a while, say for repairs. Or we have a use case **Manage Book Transfers**; are there transfers that would possibly place a book out of circulation entirely for a time, this would in effect be moving a book from region 2 to 8?

Regions 7 and 8 therefore are a reminder that such types and status of books exist, and region 7 in particular reminds us that with a little brainstorming we might envision failure scenarios that warrant error testing.

*FROM VENN DIAGRAM TO STATE TRANSITION DIAGRAM*

One last way to brainstorm using our Venn diagram of Figure 9-1: build a state transition diagram describing how a book or books would move between the regions of the Venn diagram (for a refresher on state transition testing refer back to Chapter 3 Upping the Rigor with a State Transition Diagram).

Figure 9-2 shows a state transition diagram for the valid regions (as opposed to regions that represent failure scenarios) of the Venn diagram of Figure 9-1. Such a state transition diagram can be used for test design[118], or simply to sanity check our understanding of the regions of the Venn diagram and how the use case being modeled fits into the bigger picture. Our **Return Books** use case "happy path" we have modeled in this section would be responsible for the transition of books from region 3 (books are lent) to region 1 (books are being returned), and finally to region 2 (books are again available), shown with bold arrows.

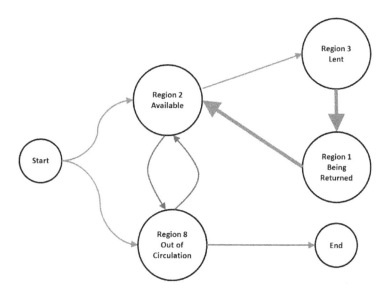

Figure 9-2 State transition diagram based on regions of the Venn diagram

---

[118] What is the cyclomatic complexity of the graph? Three regions plus one is four. So four is the upper bound on tests needed for edge coverage, the exact number for basis path coverage, and the lower bound for all paths coverage.

## BINARY RELATIONS

Binary relations over sets are a meat and potatoes topic in what Jorgensen has called *discrete math for testers.*[119],[120] For testers, binary relations are important because they are ubiquitous and have properties that we can test for. If we can say, *'Oh, this use case operation is creating (or reading, updating or deleting) this such-and-such kind of relation.."* then we immediately have at our disposal properties associated with that kind of relation which form the basis for tests.

Without resorting to discrete math to describe what a binary relation is (see Jorgensen's book), the easiest way to describe binary relations is with an example.

Let's say we are dealing with an HR management system. One of the things the system tracks is employees and departments, e.g. sales, marketing, information technology (IT), project management office, and even HR itself. Let's model these as the following two sets:

> Employees - the set of employees in the company
> Departments - the set of departments in the company

An obvious thing that an HR system will want to track is which employees work in what departments. That we model with a binary relation. Again, we'll borrow some notation from Z to describe such a relation. The following simply says that *WorksIn* is a relation describing which employees work in what departments:

> WorksIn: Employees ↔ Departments

All binary relations have two properties of interest for testing: *cardinality* and *participation.*[121] Let's look at these one at a time using our example.

---

[119] Paul Jorgensen, *Software Testing: A Craftsman's Approach*, Discrete Math for Testers
[120] Technically a relation is defined as a set, i.e. a set of tuples. In turn graphs, e.g. control flow graphs which you've already seen previously in the book, can be viewed as relations. So it's set theory from the ground up!
[121] Jorgensen, *Software Testing: A Craftsman's Approach*

The cardinality of a binary relation refers to the number of elements of one set that can be mapped to the other. There are four possible cases for any binary relationship. Continuing with our HR example:

- many to many – in our example, this would mean many employees can work in a department, and a given employee may work in many different departments.
- many to one – this would mean many employees can work in a department, but any given employee may only work in one department.
- one to many – this would mean an employee could work in many departments, but each department would be limited to a single employee.
- one to one – in this situation an employee would work in one department, and every department would have at most one employee.

The participation of a binary relation refers to whether every element of each set is *required* to be related to some element(s) of the other; i.e. is it mandatory or optional to participate in the relation. As with cardinality, there are four possible cases for any binary relationship. Using our HR example to illustrate:

- mandatory-mandatory – this would mean that all employees have to be working in a department, and that all departments have to have at least one employee assigned to work in them.
- mandatory-optional – this means that all employees have to be working in a department, but we might have a department to which no employees are assigned (perhaps allowed temporarily).
- optional-mandatory – this indicates some employees may not be assigned to work in a department, but all departments have to have at least one employee working in each.
- optional-optional – this would mean we might have employees not assigned to work in a department, and departments to which no employees have been assigned to work.

Are you seeing the power of modeling with binary relations in terms of the questions they lead us to ask?

Let's run through some examples of how we can use cardinality and participation in test design. These tricks for spotting testing opportunities are similar to those for avoiding insertion, update, and deletion "anomalies" (read bugs) in relational database design.[122] That's no coincidence. This is a handy place to re-apply C.R.U.D. thinking: think in terms of classifying use case operations in terms of whether they Create, Read, Update, or Delete the relation. It's a good way to brainstorm test design with relation cardinality and participation.

### BRAINSTORMING TESTS FROM RELATION CARDINALITY

Any relation whose cardinality involves "many" calls for test cases that demonstrate the system supports that cardinality. And of course "many" always begs the question, "How many?!" which is the basis for boundary value tests.

Any relation whose cardinality involves "one" has a constraint that serves as a precondition for any use case operation that is creating, reading, updating or deleting that relation. Violated preconditions are, as previously discussed, a basis for possible system failure, and hence may warrant error handling tests.

For example, let's take *WorksIn* and assume that we are dealing with an HR system where the *WorksIn* relation is many-to-one: many employees can work in a department, but any given employee may only work in one department:

### WorksIn: Employees ← many to one → Departments

This would tell us, as testers, that a precondition for a use case operation that involved adding an employee to a department, would be that the employee was not already in another department. So a good error test would be to try to add an employee to a department when the employee was already working in another department.

Here's an example from our library management system. Our system has a set of books (physical copies), and a set of titles, and a use case that reads the library

---

[122]Reingruber & Gregory, *The Data Modeling Handbook: A Best-Practice Approach to Building Quality Data Models*

database to produce a report. So here we build a quick model of the relation between physical books and their titles. The relation is *many to one*: many physical books have the same title, but a given book can have only one title.

This then is the precondition – actually a global invariant – for any use case that needs to read data that concerns this relationship: A book should be associated with only one title. If that precondition is violated, the read operation could well wind up reporting the wrong title for a book!

TitleOfBook: Books ← many to one → Titles

### BRAINSTORMING TESTS FROM RELATION PARTICIPATION

Any relation whose participation is "optional" calls for a test to demonstrate the system supports that participation. Let's say that for our library management system example, book participation is mandatory, but title participation is optional. In other words, every book must have a title, but it is possible to have titles of books for which we have no physical copies (yet):

TitleOfBook: Books ← mandatory optional → Titles

This would suggest tests to demonstrate the ability to support having a title without any associated physical books: Can a use case create a title without having a physical copy? Can a use case read (e.g. running a report) a title without a physical book without blowing up or displaying garbage? Can a use case update a title without an associated physical copy of the book? Can a use case delete a title without an associated book?

Any relation whose participation involves "mandatory" will have constraints use case operations will have to honor. Let's assume that in our HR system, *WorksIn* is mandatory participation for employees, but optional for departments, i.e. every employee should be working in some department, but we may have a department that is devoid of employees (perhaps being formed, or being phased out).

WorksIn: Employees ← mandatory optional → Departments

What implication will this have for use cases? Let's run through our C.R.U.D. scenarios.

A postcondition for any use case operation that adds (creates) a new employee would be that the employee is assigned to an existing department. A use case that reported on employees (read) would have as a precondition that all employees are assigned to a department. If this were missing, it might cause an error, or junk to be displayed in the report; this may warrant error testing. A use case that transfers an employee to another department (update) would have as a precondition that the employee was in another department from which to be transferred, and then as a postcondition that upon completion is in another existing department (the employee is not left unassigned to a department as part of the transfer). Finally, a precondition for a use case operation that deleted a department would be that no employees were working in that department (e.g. they should have been transferred to another department first). To delete a department with employees still in it would leave employees with no department, a violation of the mandatory participation.

## *CARTOON ANALYSIS TOOL*
Figure 9-3 illustrates a cartoon analysis tool format I find helpful (great for drawing on whiteboards during a brainstorming session) to think through all the questions we need to ask about a relation's cardinality and participation, and the tests that are suggested based on the answers.

Every binary relation has four sets of questions to be asked about the cardinality and participation of each of the two sets in the relation.

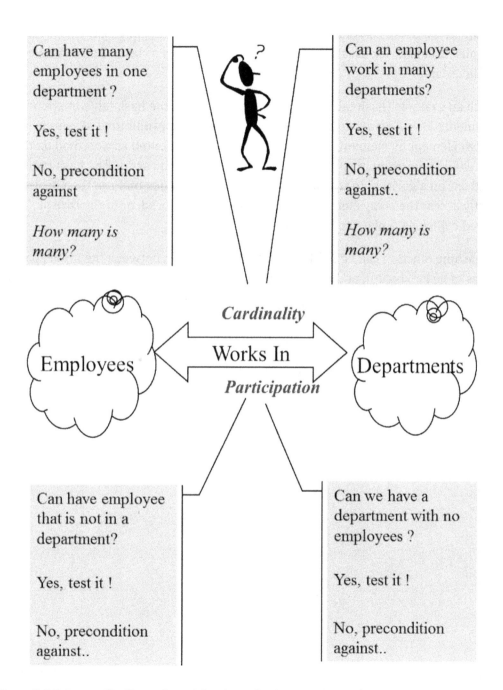

Figure 9-3 Using cardinality and participation to brainstorm in test design

Do keep in mind, binary relations are *not* just applicable to databases. Here's an example. Brian Marick uses a hash table, implemented as a class, as an example for class invariants.[123]

In such an example (hash table implemented as a class), the hash table might be implemented as an array, possibly quite large and hence prohibitive to search through element by element. A hashing function, implemented as a method on the class, would take as input something to be looked up in the array. The hash function would use an algorithm to transform the input into an index that can then be used to directly access the array element where some value is stored, or in the case of allowed collisions, a place to begin the search.

The hashing function can be modeled as a binary relation between the input space (things to be looked up), and the elements of the array. The properties of that binary relation – cardinality and participation – are the basis for the class invariant. Figure 9-4 illustrates use of the cartoon analysis format asking all the pertinent questions about the relation between inputs and array elements of the hash table. It's a good brainstorming exercise to envision different hash table implementations for various answers to these questions, and the tests that would be needed for each.

---

[123] Brian Marick, *The Craft of Software Testing*

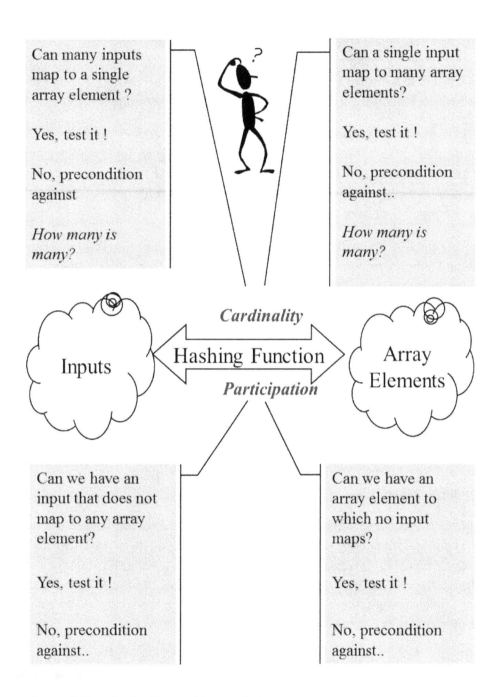

Can many inputs map to a single array element ?

Yes, test it !

No, precondition against

*How many is many?*

Can a single input map to many array elements?

Yes, test it !

No, precondition against..

*How many is many?*

*Cardinality*

Inputs    Hashing Function    Array Elements

*Participation*

Can we have an input that does not map to any array element?

Yes, test it !

No, precondition against..

Can we have an array element to which no input maps?

Yes, test it !

No, precondition against..

Figure 9-4 Modeling a hash table as a binary relation

Do you feel like you spend a good deal of your life in lines? Lines – or queues as they are referred to in software systems -- are everywhere: the freeway, grocery store, doctor's office, embarking and debarking airlines and cruise ships, banks, etc.

Queues are just as ubiquitous in computing. While queuing theory is a whole discipline of study in its own right we as testers can easily re-apply what we know about binary relations to help brainstorm tests around use cases that involve queues. For an example, we only have to look as far as our library management system where all the use cases interact with a queue.

Remember the C.R.U.D. matrix of Figure 1-5? The data entity Reservation Requests is a queue of library patrons that are waiting for a copy of a book, for example when all copies of a title are checked out. Looking at the matrix of Figure 1-5 we see that every use case either creates, reads, updates or deletes data from that queue.

OK, let's see how to re-apply what we've learned about binary relations to brainstorm tests for queues and sequences.

## Queues As Sequences
A queue is a sequence of things that form a waiting line. The keyword here is *sequence*. In mathematics a sequence is formally defined as a function. And as testers, aren't we lucky that a function is in turn defined as a binary relation! We can reuse tricks for binary relations to brainstorm tests for anything that we can model as a queue or sequence.

A sequence over a set of things is defined by mapping the set of things to the set of non-zero natural numbers, i.e. {1,2,3 ... }. It's like when you go to your favorite restaurant and there's a waiting list, you are assigned a number ( Mr. Denney, you are fifth on the waiting list! ). So that set of people milling randomly about the lobby, bar and outside the restaurant are, despite the lack of an apparent line, actually in a queue by virtue of the fact they have been assigned a number.

What I like to do for brainstorming is break from convention a bit, and think about sequences not just in terms of functions (functions are a restricted form of binary relations) but rather in terms of binary relations in general.

228

Formal definitions aside, this will make more sense with examples. Let's first run through several examples of everyday queues and sequences to see how we can use our questions about cardinality and participation to brainstorm test ideas. Then we'll return to our library management system example.

## Example: Employee Numbers as a Sequence

Because queues are defined in terms of sequences, let's start with an example of a sequence.

Earlier we saw examples of relations associated with an HR management system that tracked employees and departments. Let's continue with that example to illustrate sequences.

When employees are hired at a company, they are generally assigned employee numbers, which may even appear on the badge worn around the building. I've worked at companies where folks with single digit numbers, founders of the company, were still around. A definite status symbol!

If we want to brainstorm tests for any use case that involves employee numbers we only need to recognize that employee numbers are a sequence. We could model them like this:

$$\text{EmployeeNumber: Employees} \leftrightarrow \{1,2,3...max\}$$

In words, employee numbers are a binary relation mapping employees in the company onto a set of numbers. Now all we have to do is brainstorm using the questions we need to ask about any and every binary relation (refer back to cartoon analysis tool of Figure 9-3 for a refresher on the questions).

### Cardinality Question One: Employee Number Example
First question: Can many employees have the same employee number?

Stop! Before you answer "No" (most likely your *first* impression; certainly mine), this is an example of where I encourage you to use the questions as a way to *brainstorm* and *think outside the box*. In doing so you may well spot vagaries with the requirements and / or important tests.

229

Postponing quick judgment is a cardinal rule in brainstorming, e.g. in JAD[124] workshops. For testers, postponing quick judgment and brainstorming is, I think, a healthy approach to failure analysis.

So let's brainstorm a bit. What if the HR management system is restricted to, say, three digit employee numbers. Even though HR may never plan on having more than 999 employees, over time, as staff come and go, it may be necessary to re-cycle old employee numbers (Ouch, hadn't thought about that). If all employees, current and past, are maintained in the HR database (likely), then it could well be that at some point two employees (i.e. two persons with records still being tracked in the HR database) might have the same number.

So whatever the answer – yes or no – are you seeing how using these questions are a healthy way to identify potential requirement problems and point to tests?

*Cardinality Question Two: Employee Number Example*
Next question: Can many employee numbers be assigned to the same employee?

Again, my first instinct is to answer "No!". But let's pause and brainstorm. Can we envision a scenario where an employee might have two employee numbers? If an employee leaves a company, and then subsequently returns, say a few years later, does that employee get a new employee number? Or do they get their old employee number back? I worked at a company where a particular employee had actually done that over three times!

Once again, a scenario that leads us to ask for clarification on requirements, and whose answer points to needed tests either way!

*Participation Question One: Employee Number Example*
Next let's ask about participation in the relationship. Are all employees required to have an employee number? If so that's certainly an invariant (and hence a precondition and/or postcondition as the case may be) that any use case will need to take into account.

---

[124] Wood and Silver, Joint Application Development, 2nd 1995

Brainstorming though, can we summon up a scenario where an employee might not get an employee number? Maybe temporary employees? Even if we decide (or HR decides) that yes, even temporary employees must have an employee number, by brainstorming, we've identified a possible test we might like to run for a use case that is creating, reading, updating or deleting employee number information.

There's probably a good chance employee numbers for temporary employees would be different from regular employees. Once you make that leap, you might even start thinking about all employee numbers of all sorts!

That's the nature of brainstorming; *you sometimes get to the right answer for the wrong reason*, but it stills provides insight into things to test.

### Participation Question Two: Employee Number Example

Do all employee numbers have to be assigned to an employee? At the risk of sounding like a broken record, my immediate inclination is to say "Of course!".

Answering this question really requires us to ask questions about the set of employee numbers; Is there really a fixed set of them (remember the scenario where only 3 digits were planned for the employee number?) or are we able to use as many digits as we like (Hey, that sounds like a test).

So let's say we consider the relation to be over just employee numbers that have already been issued, putting aside the question of employee numbers for some time far in the future. Is there a way we can imagine where we might have a previously assigned employee number *not* assigned an employee? What about the scenario of the person who leaves the company, but then returns? If they are issued a new employee number, what happens to the old one? And what then happens if some reporting use case tries to use an old employee number to look up information about the employee?

Binary relations are a very simple, easy way to model things in your system that are sequences, and I think this example is a good one to illustrate problems we might not immediately recognize as being a sequence.

**Example: Ship's Tender Queue**

Binary relations can be used to model queues by virtue of the fact that a queue is a sequence of things that form a waiting line.

If you have ever taken a cruise, you are likely familiar with a ship's tender. Big cruise lines often are unable to dock close to land. So to go ashore, you queue up for a ship's tender, a small boat that shuttles people to shore. Rather than actually forming a line, passengers get a number that puts you in line ( Now you are free to go to the bar and get a fruity drink while waiting! ).

We can model this queue as a relation between passengers on the cruise, and scheduled ship tender departures throughout the day (e.g. 8AM, 8:30AM, 9AM, 9:30AM, 10AM, ... ):

$$\text{Ship's Tender: Passengers} \leftrightarrow \text{Scheduled Ship Tenders}$$

Now let's ask our standard questions about relation cardinality and participation that any tender management system would need to deal with.

*Cardinality Question One: Ship's Tender Example*

Can many passengers be assigned to the same scheduled ship tender? Given the tender boat carries more than one person, yes! And when we see "many", we can ask How many?

Our tender management system might have a minimum number of persons that need to be on the boat to make the trip worthwhile.  It surely has a maximum number. Both min and max provide boundary value tests. The maximum in particular will be the basis for a precondition on any use case adding passengers to a tender (i.e. to ensure the addition of more people does not exceed the max limit) and a boundary value test of the maximum.

*Cardinality Question Two: Ship's Tender Example*

Can a passenger be assigned to multiple tenders? Let's brainstorm. One might imagine a ship's tender management system that allowed passengers to book multiple tenders to shore for the day (You plan on going ashore early this morning, returning to the ship for lunch, and then going out again for your snorkeling tour at 3pm, all of which you'd like to book at one time).

If this is to be allowed, one would certainly need to test this. If it is prohibited, it would be, for example, a precondition for a use case adding a passenger to a tender (passenger can't already by scheduled for departure on another tender without first returning to the ship).

### Participation Question One: Ship's Tender Example

Is every passenger required to be assigned a tender? Again, stop and brainstorm. Perhaps there are different categories of tendering: voluntary (ports of call), and mandatory (evacuations!). You may have just stumbled onto two separate use cases for the tender management system.

Or maybe the tender management system has a "null tender" as a way of making sure every passenger says yes or no. Not going ashore? You need to sign up for the null tender. Improves accountability if that's important.

Either way – passengers are or aren't required assignment to a tender boat – we've identified tests to be run by simply asking the standard questions that are associated with all binary relations.

### Participation Question Two: Ship's Tender Example

How about participation of scheduled tenders: Is every scheduled launch of a tender boat required to have passengers assigned?

What happens when nobody signs up for a tender boat, say the one scheduled to leave at 5AM?! Does the tender sail for shore as scheduled, or are we know dealing with a new use case, i.e. the *Cancel Scheduled Tender* use case? Assuming passengers were the primary reason for the scheduled tender, the latter makes sense.

So if yes, participation of scheduled tenders is mandatory, this might well be a precondition for some use cases of the tender management system, e.g. the use case giving the OK for a tender to launch as scheduled.

**Example: Return Books Use Case, Reservation Requests Queue**

Let's conclude our look at binary relations for brainstorming tests for sequences and queues by returning to our library management system example.

In Chapter 2's Risk Exposure and Data, we identified Reservation Requests as high risk, based on the criteria outlined in that chapter. Also in Chapter 2, Finding the High Traffic Use Cases in Your System, we determined the **Return Books** use case to be one of the most frequently used use cases in the system.

A set of pending Reservation Requests for a particular book (library patrons waiting for that book, because for example, all copies are checked out) can be modeled as a queue, so let's brainstorm tests for a Reservation Requests queue from the perspective of the **Return Books** use case.

Figure 9-5 shows the basic flow for the **Return Books** use case (a description of all use cases for the library management system is available in Chapter 1, Use Case Descriptions via the C.R.U.D. Matrix).

Use Case: **Return Book**

> Return of a lent book or books to the library

Basic Flow

- Person brings book(s) to the library and returns them to a librarian at the customer service desk
- Librarian logs into system (if not already logged in).
- For each book, the librarian scans the book's bar code which identifies the book and borrower. System displays name of book and borrower to librarian.
- Librarian asks borrower if they are that person (or if not, are they are returning the book on behalf of that person). Librarian confirms the title of the book matches what the system displays. This serves as a cross-check that we have the right book and check out record.
- System prompts librarian to confirm they are ready to proceed with check-in; Librarian clicks enter.

- System updates the check out request for this book to show it has been returned.
- System checks for reservation requests for this book title. If reservation requests are pending, the "next in line" is flagged causing the patron to be notified that a copy is now available for pickup.

Figure 9-5 Basic Flow for Return Books Use Case

As part of the process of a book being checked back into the library, the system performs a check of pending reservation requests for the book. This operation is initiated in step #7 of the use case. The set of pending reservation requests represents a queue of patrons waiting to check out the book.

## Please Take a Number!

Each book's reservation queue will be implemented based on a circular queue, a popular approach for implementing queues in software systems. A good example of a circular queue we are all familiar with is the "take a number" system popular at post offices, pharmacies and other retail stores.

"Take a number" systems, like the one shown in Figure 9-6, rely on a paper tape (the dispenser labeled "Please take a number") with perforated tabs that can be pulled off. Each tab has printed on it a number. In the example of Figure 9-6 the tabs are labeled in order 01, 02, 03 .. up to 99. After reaching 99, the tape then repeats the sequence, 01, 02, 03 .. 99. This sequence repeats itself over and over. That's the "circular" part of the queue.

When a customer wants to "get in line", they simply pull the next tab off the tape. The number printed on the tab identifies their spot in line.

The other bit of the "take a number" system is a display that says which number is currently being served. In Figure 9-6 that's the display that says "Now Serving 99", i.e. the customer holding the tab labeled "99" is currently being served. Once that customer has been served, they pitch their paper tab in the trash, and leave. They've just left the queue! Now the clerk (let's say at the post office) is ready to help the next customer, so they advance the display to the next number in sequence ("Next customer, please."). Again, when the display reaches 99, it then goes back to 01, then 02, etc.

The library management system is going to implement its book reservation queues like a "take a number" system. We can model such a queue for any particular book as a binary relation like:

$$BookReservationQueue: PatronsWaitingOnBook \leftrightarrow \{1,2,3\ ..99\}$$

Each book reservation queue will of course need to have a "Now Serving" pointer to show who is next in line for the book. We can model this as a simple integer chosen from the set of numbers 1 through 99:[125]

$$NowServing: \{1,2,3\ ..99\}$$

---

[125] Again, borrowing notation from the specification language Z. The ":" can be read like "is a member of the set", so in our example, NowServing is a member of the set {1,2,3..99}

Now let's ask the standard questions about cardinality and participation in BookReservationQueue we can ask of any binary relation.

*Cardinality Question One: Reserve Book Example*
First, can many library patrons be assigned the same number?

We've already seen an example of such a queue, the ship's tender in the previous example. But in this case, a mapping of many patrons to a single number is prohibited. This then will be a precondition for step #7 of the use case (if you are skipping around, refer back to Chapter 8, Sanity Check Before Proceeding for why preconditions are being treated at the operation level).

If this precondition were violated, what might be the consequence to the **Return Books** use case? Since several patrons would have the same number, the notification might, e.g. be sent to multiple persons. Definitely disgruntled library customers would be involved, so the system needs to check that this precondition holds (no two patrons have the same number) before step #7. And of course we've just identified a test we'll need to run: to confirm the system correctly catches this problem should it occur.

*Take Advantage of Serendipitous Discoveries*
This is a good time to stop and point out that in working with properties of the data, e.g. modeling data with binary relations as we are doing here, an issue identified in the context of working on one use case may well point to needed tests with other use cases.

This makes sense when you look at a C.R.U.D. matrix like that of Figure 1-6. A given data entity like Reservation Requests is a common thread connecting all the use cases of the system. A data invariant that translates to a precondition for one use case probably translates to similar preconditions for other use cases.

To illustrate, let's take a second and brainstorm: In a "take a number" system, how might two patrons wind up with the same number? Thinking in terms of boundary value tests, what would happen if *more* than 99 patrons were in line for a book (the latest *Harry Potter* book for example!). Well, the 100th patron would be re-assigned the number 1, the 101st patron would be re-assigned the number 2, and so on.

In other words, if the queue grows too long, *we start re-using numbers prematurely!* The circular queue assumes that service of the queue keeps ahead of arrivals.

*Ouch*! That's definitely a problem. So the system needs to make sure it never queues more than 99 patrons for a book. This translates into a testable precondition for use case **Reserve Books**: before queuing patrons, confirm the queue is not already full!

So the same data invariant – many patrons cannot be assigned the same number in line – translates into a test for use case **Return Books** (check for the problem), and into a test for use case **Reserve Books** (prevent the problem).

*Cardinality Question Two: Reserve Book Example*
So we've seen that we have a testable condition around many patrons being assigned the same number. Can multiple numbers (1,2,3,..) be assigned to a single patron?

Let's brainstorm a bit and reflect what type of other queue might have such a property? A doctor's appointment management system would probably have such a queue. It would be quite reasonable for a each patient (waiting to see the doctor) to have multiple appointments in the future booked.

But what about the book reservation queue? After a bit of discussion with the development team and product managers, the decision is made this would not be a good idea for book reservations; It has the potential for abuse. For example, say a book is required for some class at the local college. Joe student has the great idea that rather than buying the book, why not just submit 20 reservations for the book at the local library!

So a precondition for step #7 is that many numbers in line cannot be assigned to a single patron. A consequence of this precondition being violated is the Joe student example. It is probably worth tests to demonstrate that the system does not allow a patron to do this, and that if it inadvertently happens, the system will "fail safe", e.g. the **Return Books** use case catches it before telling Joe student it's his book again for another two weeks!

In summary, the relation between patrons and positions in the waiting line is one-to-one.

*Participation Question One: Reserve Book Example*
Let's now ask questions of participation of the Book Reservation Queue relation:

$$\text{BookReservationQueue: PatronsWaitingOnBook} \leftrightarrow \{1,2,3\ ..99\}$$

Are all patrons that are waiting on a book required to have a number assigned? Sounds like a good idea. This then will be a precondition for step #7 of the **Return Books** use case. If the precondition is violated, we've got a situation where a patron is in unknown position in the queue.

*Participation Question Two: Reserve Book Example*
Is it required that all positions of the queue, numbers {1,2,3 …99}, be assigned to some patron?

We've seen one queue – the ship's tender – where, because a scheduled tender did not have any passengers, it caused a deviation from normal course (a scheduled tender with no passengers should probably be cancelled; See ship's tender example).

In the case of our "take a number" style book reservation system however, having 99 people waiting for a book is probably an exception rather than the norm. So no, participation of all numbers in the relation is not mandatory.

So while mandatory participation of all numbers is not a precondition, optional participation of numbers suggests tests we may want to consider for the **Return Books** use case. Are we able to return books with no patrons in the reservation queue? Books with some, but less than a full queue of patrons? How about a full queue?

All three cases are likely to execute different paths through the code. The second scenario – some patrons, but not a full queue – can be further subdivided into to cases: patrons occupying contiguous positions in the queue (five patrons waiting on the book with assigned numbers 4, 5, 6, 7, 8) and patrons occupying *non-contiguous* positions in the queue. This is a situation created when a person in the middle of the queue changes their mind and cancels their reservation; We'd like to ensure that the code properly recognizes that a position in line has been vacated by a canceled reservation, doesn't "blow up", and correctly continues past that position to find the next inline.

## UNARY RELATION (A SPECIAL TYPE OF BINARY RELATION!)

There is another type of relation that has properties that can be tested. It's called a unary relation. It's like a binary relation, but where the "two sets" are actually the same set.

Because a unary relation is as a binary relation between elements of a single set, it has all the testable properties of any binary relation. But because it is a relation over a single set, it has additional properties that a tester can utilize.

Let's take an example and begin with the properties of a binary relation, and show how they still apply to unary relations.

### *CARDINALITY AND PARTICIPATION IN A UNARY RELATION*

In the previous section we used the example of an HR management system and the tracking of which employees worked in what departments. The system might also need to track who works for whom. And again we can model this with a binary relation, but this time over just the set of employees:

### WorksFor: Employees ↔ Employees

As a binary relation, we can ask all the questions one can ask of any binary relation in terms of cardinality and participation as illustrated in Figure 9-7.

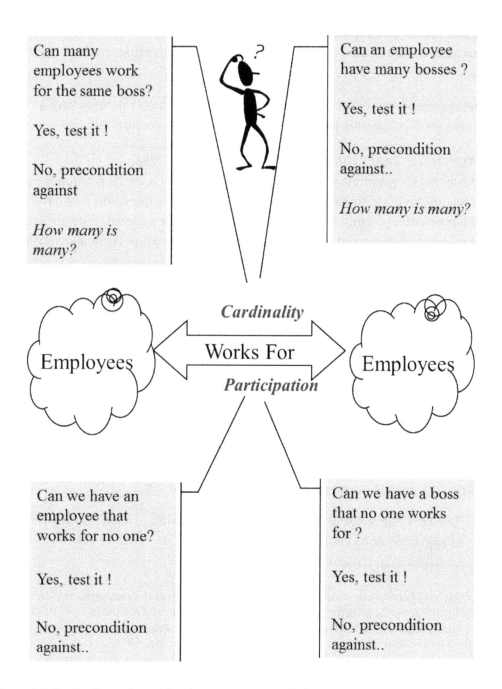

Figure 9-7 Cardinality and participation questions to ask about the *WorksFor* relation

It's a good brainstorming exercise to envision different supervisory setups for the various answers to the questions of Figure 9-7 and the tests that would be needed for each.

Beyond the properties of cardinality and participation, unary relations have an additional set of properties we as testers can leverage. Let's turn to those.

### ADDITIONAL TESTABLE PROPERTIES OF UNARY RELATIONS

In addition to the questions of cardinality and participation, if the relation is over a single set, we have additional questions we can ask. These questions relate to testable properties of a unary relation, namely reflexivity, symmetry, transitivity, and one less often discussed, but which I find helpful, the property of allowing cycles:

- Reflexivity: can an element be related to itself, e.g. in terms of our HR management system example, can an employee be their own boss?
- Symmetry: if Bob works for Carol, does Carol also work for Bob?
- Transitivity: if Allen works for Bob, and Bob works for Carol, does Allen then work for Carol as well?
- Cycles: If Allen works for Bob, and Bob work Carol, can Carol work for Allen?

While books on discrete math generally approach these topics in terms of defining what it means for a relation *to be* reflexive, symmetric or transitive, for purposes of testing I prefer to ask the question from a slightly different slant: Are occurrences of reflexivity, symmetry, transitivity, and cycles *prohibited*: [126]

- Does the relation *prohibit* an element being related to itself? Such a relation is said to be *Anti-reflexive*.

---

[126] Terminology here can be muddy. The terms anti-reflexive, anti-symmetric, anti-transitive and acyclic are about as unambiguous as I've found in the literature. Note however that uses of the terms irreflexive, asymmetric and intransitive may or may not mean the same thing depending on the source. Note also, *not* reflexive/symmetric/transitive does not mean anti-reflexive/symmetric/transitive. "Anti-" is a stronger statement meaning it is prohibited. Not reflexive e.g. doesn't rule out an element being related to itself, just that it's not universally taken to hold in the relation. Hence my preference for "anti-". It's meaning is unambiguous and amounts to a data invariant which can be tested.

- If A is related to B, does the relation *prohibit* B being related to A? Such a relation is said to be *Anti-symmetric*.
- If A is related to B, and B is related to C, does the relation *prohibit* A being related to C? Such a relation is said to be *Anti-transitive*.
- If A is related to B, and B is related to C, does the relation *prohibit* C from being related to A? Such a relation is said to be *Acyclic*.

So why are these questions useful from a test design perspective? Because the answer either way – yes it's prohibited, or no it's allowed -- points to possible tests we may need to consider.

If the relation *prohibits* the occurrence, we've just identified a precondition for any use case operation that creates, reads, updates or deletes the relation. We may want a failure test based on the violated precondition.

On the other hand, if the relation *allows* the occurrence we've just identified a (non-failure) test case we probably need to try, e.g. the test of a use case creating, reading, updating or deleting an employee who is their own boss!

Let's take some examples of unary relationships and try asking these four questions.

The relation "Nominates" as in a system that maintains (i.e. creates, reads, updates, deletes) tracking of persons nominating other persons, e.g. for some office or position:

- Reflexivity – Prohibited; one can't nominate oneself. Precondition against this.
- Symmetry – Allowed; two people might well nominate each other, and certainly a case worth testing
- Transitivity – Prohibited; person A can nominate B, and B could nominate C, but that does not imply A has also nominated C, nor would it be allowed for A to (also) nominate C (one can only nominate one other person). Precondition against this.
- Cyclic – Allowed; A nominates B, B nominates C, C nominates A. Another worthwhile test.

243

The relation "Occurs Before" as in a system that maintains relations between chronological events:

- Reflexivity – Prohibited; an event can't occur before itself. Precondition against creating, reading, updating or deleting any relation like this.
- Symmetry – Prohibited; two events can't occur before one another (considerations of relativity aside!). Precondition against this.
- Transitivity – Allowed. If event A occurs before B, and B before C, then it would be permissible for the system to infer A was also before C (a testing opportunity), and/or to allow a use case to establish or maintain a direct relation between the two.
- Cyclic – Prohibited; for same reason as prohibition on symmetry.

The relation "Replacement For" as in a system that maintains the tracking of part types that are replacements for other part types:

- Reflexivity – Allowed; a part can certainly be replaced by another part of the same type. This is a case where the relation is fully reflexive, i.e. all elements of the set meet this criteria.
- Symmetry – Allowed; two parts may well be interchangeable. Other parts may not be; Both cases are worthwhile tests to make sure the system is not assuming that because A is a replacement for B, that B is automatically a replacement for A.
- Transitivity – Allowed; it is conceivable that part A is a replacement for B, B for C, and that in turn A can be used as a replacement for C. This is good illustration of a case where the relation is *not* transitive in the formal sense (transitivity is not universal), nor is it anti-transitive (not prohibited). Implementation wise, the system would need a way to know when transitivity was allowed or not. Definitely a worthwhile test.
- Cyclic – Allowed; A is a replacement for B, B for C, and C for A.

*DO BOOK SEARCH USE CASE EXAMPLE*

Recall back in Chapter 2, section Timeboxing: Budgeting Test Design Time, we discussed a strategy of budgeting time in test design to focus on those use cases most frequently used. That way if we run out of allotted time to write tests, we've tackled the use cases that are going to take the biggest beating by the user.

Given **Do Book Search** use case accounted for about 44% relative frequency in our operational profile (refer back to Figure 2-9) we've been designing lots of test for it:

- In Chapter 4, section Control Flow Graphs: Adjusting the Rigor of Test Design, we looked at designing tests for this use case using "happy path", node, edge and basis path coverage.
- Later in Chapter 6, Example 2: Syntax Testing for Do Book Search Use Case, we used syntax testing to design tests for the input to the keyword search.

Now let's turn to applying what we've learned about brainstorming tests using unary relations to this same use case.

One of the steps in that test case (Figure 4-4) was to perform a book search based on title:

- Test step: User types *keywords from the title of a book* that is known to exist in the library database.
- Expected result: System finds all books with titles that contain the keywords, and displays them in list form.

Let's say a late breaking requirement for this use case is that in addition to displaying direct matches, the search operation needs to show sequels to each book that matches the search query.[127]

---

[127] Realistically we'd probably also want to show prequels, and could do so by returning books for which the matching book is a sequel.

As a tester, we realize that we can model this notion of book sequels as a unary relation over books:

IsSequelTo: Books ↔ Books

Questions about properties of cardinality and participation will apply here (refer back to Binary Relations), but let's focus on the questions we as testers need to ask by virtue of this being a unary relation:

Reflexivity – Prohibited. A book cannot be the sequel to itself. Any use case operation that creates or updates book sequel information will have this property – the relation is *anti-reflexive* -- as a postcondition. The **Do Book Search** use case, as a reader of book sequel data will have as a precondition that a book is *not* showing itself as a its own sequel. Consequences of violating the precondition? One can for example imagine an infinite loop scenario that could develop.

Symmetry – Prohibited. The relation is *anti-symmetric*. The **Do Book Search** use case will have anti-symmetry as a precondition. Again one can image an infinite loop developing if this precondition fails.

Transitivity –As Alan Davis has pointed out *"Natural languages suffer from inherent ambiguity [and that] trying to construct more formal models of the requirements"* is an effective way to spot it. [128] Here's a great example of just that. By "sequel" do we mean just the *one* book immediately following another in a series? Or do we mean *all* in the series that followed a book? As an example, Larry McMurtry's "Lonesome Dove" series consists of four books: *Dead Man's Walk, Comanche Moon, Lonesome Dove, and Streets of Laredo*[129]

If the user searched on "dead man", in addition to displaying Larry McMurtry's "Dead Man's Walk", do we want the system to display just "Comanche Moon" as the

---

[128] See Principles 28 and 53, *201 Principles of Software Development* by Alan Davis.
[129] Some book trivia: Sequels are not always written in chronological order. In the example here, McMurtry's "Lonesome Dove" series, the third in the series was written first, the fourth of the series written second, the first written third, and the second written last: Dead Man's Walk (1995), Comanche Moon (1997), Lonesome Dove (1985), Streets of Laredo (1993)

sequel? Or do we want the system to display "Comanche Moon", "Lonesome Dove", and "Streets of Laredo" as sequels?

This hinges on the answer to our modeling question; Is this relation transitive?!

### IsSequelTo: Books ↔ Books

If the answer is yes, we can envision the need for tests for **Do Book Search** to make sure that with series such as Lonesome Dove, the implementation is such that multiple listings of the same book are not displayed. To illustrate, if the implementation lists the immediate sequel to a book, then recursively lists the sequels to the sequels, we would have some books repeated multiple times. In other words, the implementation has to have some "smarts" on how to handle transitivity correctly.

If the answer is no, which is to say the relation is *anti-transitive*, we can envision the need for tests for **Do Book Search** to ensure the implementation is correctly interpreting the anti-transitive property. For **Do Book Search** for example, the only sequel listed for "Dead Man's Walk" should be "Comanche Moon".

Cycles – Prohibited for the same reason as reflexivity and symmetry. That unary relation *IsSequelTo* is *acyclic* is a precondition for **Do Book Search** use case, or any use case that reads the data. Violation of the precondition could result in infinite looping. A test that ensures the system handles such a violated precondition could well be in order, i.e. books are "dummied" up to include a cycle.

For any use case that creates or updates data about book sequels, being acyclic is a postcondition, i.e. no use case should create such a cycle.

### CHAPTER REVIEW

Let's review the highpoints from this chapter.

Models play a big role in failure analysis, and in test design. In the previous chapter we began with numeric models as a simple basis to illustrate the important connection between preconditions, postconditions and invariants. That chapter concluded by expanding the modeling tool kit to include sets. In this chapter we extended the modeling tool kit further to include relations between sets. Quoting Boris Beizer *"Relations have properties and therefore can be categorized. If you can say 'Oh! This is such-and-such a kind of relation,' then whatever you know about that kind of relation in general applies to the specific case".*

Venn diagrams are a simple, yet powerful tool for expressing relations between sets. In addition to being a handy way to calculate the precondition for a specific postcondition and invariant, they are a great tool for simply brainstorming tests. To demonstrate their use, we revisited an example from the previous chapter (Example 3: Return Books Use Case) to brainstorm tests for that use case.

Binary relations over sets are a meat and potatoes topic in what Jorgensen has called *discrete math for testers*. For testers, binary relations are important because they are ubiquitous and have properties that we can test for: *cardinality* and *participation*. Using a series of examples we saw how these properties are easily applied to brainstorming tests. A simple cartoon format analysis tool was presented to help think through the four basic set of questions that a tester needs to ask about any binary relation!

Queues and sequences are ubiquitous is software applications as well. We looked at how testers can easily re-apply the questions that can be asked of all binary relations, to help brainstorm tests around use cases that involve queues and sequences.

We concluded the chapter by looking at unary relations. Because a unary relation is a binary relation between elements of a single set, it has all the testable properties of any binary relation. But because it is a relation over a single set, there are additional questions that can be asked of any unary relation, answers to which point to possible tests we may need to consider. We used these questions to define more tests for the **Do Book Search** use case.

# CONCLUSION

This book has presented a strategy for test design based on use cases combined with high bang for the buck ideas from software testing, quality function deployment (QFD), software reliability engineering's operational profiles, structured analysis and design's C.R.U.D. analysis, and formal methods like model-based specification and discrete math for testers.

We've looked at a strategy to evaluate a set of use cases for test adequacy; budget test design time to maximize reliability and minimize testing cost; strike a balance between breadth of coverage of all functionality and depth of coverage for the most frequently used, critical functionality. The strategy provides a step by step process for when to use the plethora of test techniques covered in so many testing books helping address the plea "Just tell me where to start!". And we've also introduced innovative test design techniques not covered in other testing books as well as elaborated on key techniques covered only briefly in other books.

Books, like software, get released with imperfections. I published this, the second edition, to correct defects in the first, make points I didn't feel I properly made in the first edition, smooth out the rough edges, and add new material that didn't make it into the first edition (scope control!). If you, the reader, find additional defects in this second edition, have questions, or suggestions on how to make future editions more useful, I would love to hear from you; contact information is available at the end of the book, see *ABOUT THE AUTHOR*. If you find the book helpful I'd appreciate a positive review on Amazon.

# ABOUT THE AUTHOR

Richard Denney is the author of *Succeeding with Use Cases: Working Smart to Deliver Quality*, Addison-Wesley Publishing's object-technology series.

Richard has spent over 30 years in software development and testing process management including as a principal in software process improvements for Landmark Graphics (now part of Halliburton) and Schlumberger, the oil industry's two largest suppliers of software solutions, the Texas State Office of the Attorney General, and several Fortune 500 companies as a consulting affiliate of TeraQuest Metrics (now a part of Borland Software Corporation) and SAIC. Richard has over 20 years' experience as an author, presenter, panelist and reviewer in software quality assurance / testing and software development. Richard holds a patent for the industrial application of "artificial intelligence" (logic programming).

You can reach Richard by e-mail at rdenney@utexas.edu

# INDEX

www.ingramcontent.com/pod-product-compliance
Lightning Source LLC
Chambersburg PA
CBHW080401060326
40689CB00019B/4093